CW01629655

How To Become A

Great Painter and Decorator

Orhan Mehmet

ISBN: 978-1-5272-2681-4

First published 2018

CONTENTS

Introduction

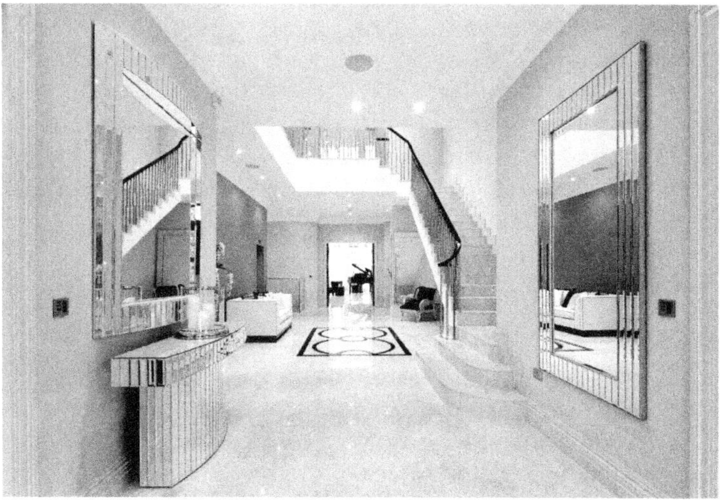

Hello there, and thank you for picking up a copy of this guide. My name is Orhan Mehmet. I'm a highly experienced painter and decorator. I also run a highly successful business. In this guide, I want to help you do the same. Using my tips and tricks, you can accelerate your career and soar to new heights.

Before we start, let me tell you a little bit more about me:

I first began painting and decorating when I was 15 years old. Now that I'm 35, with 20 years of experience to my name, it's safe to say that I know what I am talking about when it comes to this field.

In the beginning I used to work with my stepfather, Paul the "Birdman" McKracken and my uncles – Shen and Steve. I fondly remember spending summer holidays, half-terms and even some school days working with them. Naturally, they gave me all of the horrible prepping jobs, like sanding down, stripping wallpaper and sweeping up dust and muck. I swore I'd never end up doing this for a living! To be honest, without realising, I learnt so much from them including the importance of attention to detail and team work, but I never took it that seriously...but then I never really took my life too seriously at that point either.

It wasn't until the recession in 2008, when I found myself out of work, that I really hit rock bottom. As hard as I tried, I could not find work anywhere. I was on the dole for months, and slipped into a depression. I had sleepless nights, and felt helpless and useless. It was a very lonely time. Every night I'd wake up and pray around 3 or 4am, promising myself that if I got another opportunity, I'd give it 110%, and be the best that I possibly could.

Then, one day, I received a phone call. I was offered to work on a new build in Bishops Avenue, in Hampstead. This was the opportunity I'd been praying for. From that point onwards,

I was the first person in every morning. I worked the hardest, produced better finishes and became a valuable member of the company. I built an impenetrable wall of self-confidence, focus and desire to be the best at what I do. I woke up with determination, and went home with satisfaction. This is a working mentality that I have carried over to this day.

My day started at 05:30. I'd get the train to London at 06:00, get to work at 07:00 and start working. My foreman and colleagues would turn up at 08:00 to see me hard at it. The respect that I gained for this was phenomenal. I received a pay rise on my first day, then 3 more that year, making me the highest earning painter in the company.

In order to maintain this, I had to develop a strong mindset. I realised that my mentality was just as important as my ability. This is what I believe made me the most valuable painter in the company – doing more, but never asking for more in return to begin with anyway.

It wasn't long before I was promoted to foreman. Although I was very proud of how far I'd come, I soon became unsatisfied with working for an employer. I wanted more. I've never been fond of dancing to someone else's tune, but this was the first point where I really decided to take action. The long days had become unbearable, as I was only spending a couple of hours a day with my wife and son. I knew that I had to set up my own business, and be my own boss. This meant that I could take ownership of my work and have more time to see my family each day.

The final straw arrived one day at work. A song came on the radio. I'll never forget this moment, because I believe it was the defining event that pushed me into starting my own company. The song was by George Ezra, *Blame It On Me*. If you aren't familiar with the song, the singer essentially asks the listener what they are waiting for, and to get a move on with fixing their life. I didn't hang around. Later that week, I had my website made, and incorporated Trademark Decorating Services Ltd. I joined the Painting and Decorating Association, Checkatrade and Mybuilder. I remember having clients call me at work, and providing quotes for them in the evening. Eventually I had enough work coming through, and I left the company that I was working for, to focus on my own company.

Nowadays, I have so much more time in the day for my family. I wake up with them, share breakfast, and take my son to school, before heading to work. I normally get back around 4pm, and enjoy the rest of the day with my loved ones. I've honestly never been happier.

Why I wrote this book

So, why did I write this book? Put simply, I felt the need to share my experiences with others who are interested in this trade. Not only that, but I want to help others become the best they possibly could be, to guide them, and to make their journey a little easier than mine.

It's always been a personal goal of mine to write a book, and if it helps people, that'll be great.

I want this book to arm you with knowledge that you'll be able to implement immediately. It took me years to learn all that I have, but I really hope that this book can provide you with easier and more effective methods, which you can apply to this trade.

How this book will benefit YOU

Using this book, you'll benefit from amazing tips for success. These are techniques that I believe can make you either the best decorator in your company, or just help you to do a fantastic job on your properties.

Some people find painting and decorating very leisurely. I can vouch for that, as it has a calming, relaxing and satisfying effect on me...for the most part anyway! There is still the odd occasion where I feel like screaming and going crazy, but that's only because I'm a perfectionist. Not everything in life will go to plan, but if you can go home at the end of the day knowing that you've earned your pay, and done the best work possible, I'm confident that you can be as satisfied and happy as I am right now.

Now, let me briefly run through some of the tips that I'll include in this book:

- I'll demonstrate how preparing for, and planning your jobs, can make or break you.
- I'll show you the correct tools and paints to use for each job, and how to use them.
- I'll teach you how to quote, when to quote and the important legal difference between estimates and quotes. I'll also share an actual quote that I've used, to give you a detailed breakdown of what to look out for.
- I'll share where to advertise for maximum returns, and where to avoid wasting money.
- I'll give you the lowdown on what qualifications you'll need for the trade.
- I'll also give some pros and cons, to help you decide which route is best for you. We're all different. Some people like to do it for themselves, while others prefer to do it comfortably and safely within a respectable company, it's all good as long as you're happy. Whichever one of these applies to you, I'm confident I can help you.

Who is this guide for?

The experience, tips and techniques that I'll share with you within this guide will be largely aimed at 3 types of people. However, even if you aren't one of the following, then I'm confident that my advice can help you out:

- **If you are looking to paint your own property**, then this guide will be great for you. Some people have the mentality that you can teach a monkey to paint, but this just isn't true at all. In fact, I'm grossly offended by this statement, and you should be too! Painting takes great skill, and I applaud those that understand this fact and want to take the time to work on their skills and techniques.

- **If you want to train up as a painter and decorator, and work for a prestigious company**, then this guide will be great for you. With all my experience in the industry, I have a very good idea of where you can train and how to impress employers. The tips contained in this guide will show you how to maximise your skills and make yourself a valuable prospect for any employer.

- **If you are intending to start up on your own and be your own master and commander**, then this guide will be great for you. In this book you'll learn how I made the transition from working for someone else to running my own business, spending more time with my family, and even writing this book. None of these things would have been possible whilst working for someone else, because I just wouldn't have had the time!

So, with all of that being said, let's get started!

What Makes A Great Painter and Decorator?

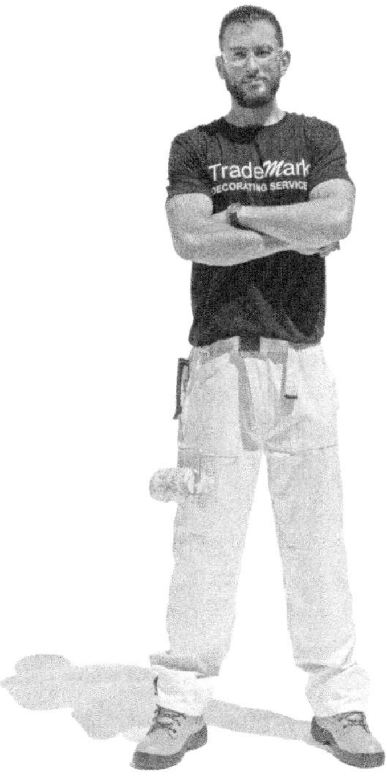

I want to start this book by covering an extremely important topic, and that is discussing what exactly makes a great painter and decorator. In my opinion, it's really important to understand exactly what qualities and aspects go into making a successful painter and decorator, before you even enter the industry. Having these aspects in your mind when you begin, will help you to behave in the correct fashion, and work in an exemplary manner.

What it takes to be a great painter and decorator

If you're aiming to become great in the painting and decorating trade, which I believe you should be, then you need to begin with improving your mindset. As I said before, your mentality is actually more important than your ability; because skill, calibre and expertise will follow after time.

There are a great number of mental traits which will help you in this trade, including taking responsibility, putting in 110% effort for your client, and applying the trade correctly – to avoid risk and damage. Over the course of this book, I will help you to see how these traits are the foundation of becoming a great painter and decorator.

Along with this, there's also another important trait that I'd like to cover, and this is **patience**. Remember that it usually takes time to produce a high-end finish, depending on the type of job or site you're working on. In patience, we find qualities such as endurance, calmness, composure, tolerance, understanding and consideration; along with kindness, perseverance, tenacity, determination and application.

Whether you already have patience, or decorating installs it into you, there's no doubt that this quality will lead you not only to become a great painter and decorator, but also to become a great leader, parent, spouse etc. Once you have developed patience, you can wake up with determination. You'll have the tolerance and composure to deal with an ungrateful boss or difficult client, have the perseverance, tenacity and endurance to get through tough times, consideration and kindness when working in people's homes, and have the calmness to apply your skill to the trade, no matter what, day-in day-out.

Now that we've looked at the mental aspects of the role, please allow me to share with you my top 25 tips for success as a painter and decorator. In my opinion, everything on this list is fundamental in making up a great tradesman.

Top 25 Tips For Success

Tip 1: Use kettle and scuttle liners

Part of being a successful painter and decorator is in managing your time and resources effectively. One of the biggest mistakes that I see newcomers to the trade make, is that they spend lots of time doing little bits of work, which could be avoided by simple planning beforehand. This means that the work goes on for longer, which can sometimes lead to an unhappy customer – along with depletion of your resources. Using liners is a very basic tip, but it will save you a lot of time washing and rinsing paint out of everything from clothes to equipment. Once you are finished painting, you can just safely dispose of the liners. Simple!

Tip 2: Stay tidy, stay organised

Being tidy and organised is one of the core requirements for any painter and decorator. It's all about efficiency. Keeping your van and tools organised will ensure that you don't have to waste time looking for a certain brush, roller, grade of sand paper, screw driver or filling knife. This can be extremely tedious and time consuming, when you could be spending your time producing great work. So, after each job, I recommend that you reorganise your tools and van, keeping your brushes, rollers and other equipment all together in a place where you can find it. The key to being a successful painter and decorator is in your ability to work in an efficient manner, whilst still producing the best possible quality.

Tip 3: Wash your tools after every use

As a painter and decorator, your tools are your livelihood. So, you need to look after them. The best way to look after your tools is to wash them out thoroughly after each use. By doing this, you can ensure that your brushes, rollers and filling knives will last for a long time, which in turn ensures a great finish and protects your reputation. Along with this, it will cost you more money to keep replacing them. So, save your hard-earned money, and keep your tools clean. Having dirty tools can also mean that your work isn't as good, since you could lose the ability to produce a great finish. Your reputation is everything in this trade, so you can't allow this to happen.

All water-based paints like emulsion, matt and silk can be cleaned from brushes and rollers with water. Oil based paints like gloss and satin are mainly used for wood and metal, and can be washed out with white spirits or paint thinners. One great tip is to leave wet brushes used with oil-based paint in a brush mate box. However, just be sure to replace the vapour pad when it runs out. Don't forget to take dust sheets down the launderette once in a while, as your customers won't like dirty smelly dust sheets in their home!

Tip 4: Use the best tools

During my time as a painter and decorator, I've seen many people try and take shortcuts, by using cheap tools. The end result of this is that their equipment wears out extremely fast, and the job that they do is ultimately nowhere near as good. In my personal experience, using the best brushes and rollers have helped me to achieve greatness. They'll last much longer, won't lose bristles, and they'll help you to cut in laser-guided straight lines. Cheap brushes will lose bristles on nearly every stroke, which in turn will leave your paintwork looking messy and unprofessional. Trust me when I say that having to remove bristles from a door that you are glossing, and getting paint in your fingernails, is not something you want to be doing.

Tip 5: Prep for the job

In this book I'm going to emphasise the importance of preparation over and over again, so let's start now. Preparation is the most important part of any decorating job! I always spend more time on preparation than actually doing the painting. This guarantees that the painting will be much easier, and also achieves a superior finish too. Prepping for the job includes using filler, scraping away flaking paint, fixing mould problems, filling or caulking gaps around windows, doors, skirting boards and sanding rough surfaces to achieve the smooth paintable surface required. All this must be completed before you even open a can of paint!

Tip 6: Quality pays

If you expect to be a great painter and decorator, then you need to use the best paints out there. I always use the trade version of the big names like Dulux, from specialist stockists rather than from retail/DIY stores. The differences in price are negligible. In my opinion, you should never buy the cheaper retail alternatives. Always get the best for your customer – because this will enhance your reputation within the industry. The trade version of paints have a lot more pigments (the coloured dyes), so will generally take 2 coats, whereas the retail alternative could take 3 maybe 4 coats. The better opacity and thickness of trade paints means more profit and a better all-round job. When we talk about opacity in paints, we refer to the ability of a coat of paint to hide the surface beneath or the previous coat of paint from view. So, the retail/DIY versions have poor opacity, and are a lot thinner. Therefore it is best to avoid them.

Tip 7: Planning for the job

We've talked about prepping, so now let's cover planning. Planning is just as important as prepping, as it can save you a lot of valuable time. As an example, imagine that you have an empty full-house redecoration job. Would you just charge blindly into this, doing everything as and when you can? No, because that would be a disaster, and your time management would be all over the place. You'd start with the ceilings, and then work your way down the walls. Once the ceilings and walls are complete then you can focus on the woodwork, which can include windows, doors, skirting boards and banisters. Some painters prefer to complete the woodwork after the ceilings, taping up the edges with low tack masking or frog tape, then completing the walls last. If the job has carpets and furniture, then you'll need to be thinking about protecting, using dust sheets, tapes, plastic drop sheets etc. I always tape up sockets, switches and skirting boards, as this protects against possible splatter from the roller and leaves a great clean edge. Make a list of all the paints and materials that you're going to be using along with making sure you have the correct tools and PPE. So, in one paragraph, you can see how we have planned out the entire structure of a job, moving from A to B to C. Planning will ultimately make your life so much easier.

Tip 8: Wear personal protective equipment (PPE)

Being a great painter and decorator involves protecting yourself at all times when on site. Accidents happen sometimes, but you must do all you can to prevent them from occurring. Wearing

PPE can really help with this. If you've taken the Construction Skills Certification Scheme (CSCS) test or gained an NVQ in painting and decorating, then you'll be familiar with this. Let's face it, you can't be great or successful if you're having injuries or accidents. I always wear safety glasses to prevent paint spray, dust or other particles injuring my eyes. If there are exposures to hazardous dusts, fumes, mists or vapours as a result of the work process, I will wear the appropriate dust mask to protect my lungs. I also wear safety boots to prevent my toes being crushed by paint tins or other heavy items, sharp items like nails penetrating the sole of my feet, or slipping on smooth or wet surfaces.

On my hands, I wear thin painter's gloves. These protect the skin on my hands from paints and other decorating substances, like white spirits, from irritation. Gloves also provide protection from sandpaper, which can leave your fingertips sore or bleeding. I wear these items everyday on residential jobs. On many sites you'll need additional PPE like hard hats and high visibility vests.

Tip 9: Understand the importance of training and learning

While I learned the trade the old-fashioned way, working with family as a school boy, I'd highly recommend taking advantage of the many apprenticeships out there nowadays. Keep up to date with the latest product innovations, new decorating techniques and industry legislation. This way you'll stay one step ahead of your competition. I've learned new tips and techniques from so many people I've worked with, in every company I've ever worked in. There's nearly always a better or more efficient way to do things. It's really amazing what having an open mind can do for you. Sometimes the people you least expect can teach you a new way of doing something. So, stay open to new ideas and improvement, and accept that you'll need to be constantly upping your game and staying ahead of the competition.

Tip 10: Ask customers where they found your details

This is especially relevant if you are running a business. Always ask your customers, even potential ones who enquire about your services, where they found your details. This way you can track which adverts are generating leads, and what isn't working. Ultimately, advertising is a trial and error process, so try everything! You need to speculate to accumulate, as the old saying goes. I've tried most things like leaflets, magazines and newspapers, but I've found personally that the majority will go online. For this reason, I focus mainly on my website, Checkatrade and Mybuilder.

Tip 11: Hire an accountant or bookkeeper

Again, focusing on the business element of things, hiring an accountant or bookkeeper is pretty much a must-do. It's nothing to be ashamed of either, we aren't all great with numbers, and even if you are experienced in this area, an accountant or bookkeeper is specially trained to assist you in this. With an experienced and professional accountant on your team, you can rest easy knowing your financial affairs are being managed by an expert. In the meantime, you can focus your attention on the important matters of the business – like finding and securing work. I used to do my own accounting, but it just got too much to handle. Trust me, an accountant or bookkeeper is well worth the money.

Tip 12: Answer calls in a professional manner

Your customer service skills are paramount in this profession. If you have poor customer service skills then you will not last long in the painting and decorating trade, as nobody wants to hire a rude or unpleasant person. When a potential customer calls you, you need to create a great first impression. Remember that this is the first point of contact, where they'll get an idea of whether they like you or not. Speak clearly and gently, with confidence, while being friendly, and set up a time to visit for a free quote.

Tip 13: Be punctual

This goes without saying. Punctuality is really important, and your reputation will really suffer if you start turning up late to jobs. Once a time has been agreed to either visit for a quote or start the actual job, always arrive on time, if not a little early. If you'll be late or need to cancel for any reason, make sure you contact the customer immediately. Your customers will appreciate this and respect you for it. Part of offering a professional and efficient service is making sure that you are there on time. This also relates to planning. If you need to travel for the job then it makes sense to plan your route beforehand, and leave with plenty of time to spare – just in case of traffic.

Tip 14: Dress appropriately

When meeting a customer for the first time, you really should try and dress as clean and smart as possible. This is especially important if you are meeting them to provide a quote. Your potential customer will be assessing whether they want you working in their home or not, so you need to make a good first impression. I'm not saying that you need to wear a tux, but you should dress smart, smell nice and look clean. This really helps to win the work, and ultimately that's what it's all about. One tip is to offer to remove your shoes on arrival. This shows that you'll respect their home and treat it as you would your own. If on the other hand you've got the job and you're just starting, then be sure to wear a clean t-shirt with your company logo showing and a pair of decorating trousers, bib and brace, or as painters call them “whites”. Don’t let them get too dirty with paint before replacing them. Just remember to be conscious of your image, because it does make a difference.

Tip 15: Join the Painting and Decorating Association (PDA)

One of the first things I did when I started my company was to join the PDA, and I’m very proud and glad that I did. Being a member of the PDA distinguishes professionals from the crowd, as we adhere to the PDA code of practice, which demonstrates commitment to professional quality workmanship and fair practice through business activities. The PDA provides access to services such as business insurance, income protection and medical care, as well as dental and personal accident insurance.

When asked about what the PDA offers, the chief executive of the organisation had the following to say:

“It gives painters and decorators a presence under the banner of Britain’s largest trade body for the industry, and allows them to combine customer reviews with information about the benefits of employing a PDA member. There’ll also be a whole range of features for members including our industry leading e-learning training package, a forum and even an online shop – so all their needs can be met in one place. Customers visiting the new website will be able to request a quote from members as well as having the chance to leave feedback- combining the popularity of review only sites with the assurance the organisation’s code of conduct and other services such as its arbitration facility. Standing for professionalism, confidence and integrity, the PDA symbol is the sign of quality in the industry. The PDA represents thousands of painters and decorators across the UK, but the association has one clear purpose – to ensure all members adhere to the highest standards. From large national contractor organisations through to small businesses - the PDA chooses its decorators with care."

So, you can see that this is a fantastic organisation to join. Here's some of the benefits:

- Free listing in the online member directory.
- PDA certification for your stationery, adverts and van.
- Free support and advice to grow your business.
- Support in undertaking industry specific training programmes.
- Influence on relevant government policy and nationally negotiated wage levels.
- Recognition of best practice through industry awards.
- Opportunity to meet fellow trade professionals.
- Free legal help.

Tip 16: Join Checkatrade

Checkatrade is one of the leading platforms for trade professionals. To be honest, it's my favourite. Since I joined Checkatrade I get enquiries all the time, as it generates by far the most leads, and a lot are actually converted into jobs I'm constantly busy. I would strongly advise you to sign up and make use of the site, as it's definitely worth the annual fee! The more jobs you win and complete, the higher the scores you receive from feedback that your customers leave. Following that, you'll get even more calls and enquiries, and start to really grow your business.

Tip 17: Don't chase the money

I think this is a really important tip, and it's one that a lot of people will probably struggle to come to terms with. We're all obviously in this to make money, but if you only think about the money then you're more likely to struggle when things get difficult. For example, if a job doesn't go the way you planned. This happens a lot too. If you instead focus on doing a great job, no matter what, you'll achieve an amazing finish – resulting in a very happy customer who'll leave you a glowing review and top marks. I seriously can't stress this enough. The most important thing is a happy customer. One happy customer can lead to two happy customers, and two to three, and so on.

Tip 18: Care for your customers

Similarly to the last tip, I think it's vital that you can show a level of care and appreciation for your customers. I personally care deeply about the work I do and the happiness of my customers. My customers have trusted me to decorate their homes and properties. So, the least I can do is care about the work I produce. It's not enough for me to just leave my customers 'satisfied', they must be so happy and impressed that they'll leave me great feedback and score me 10/10! If you don't care about your customers then you'll never be a great painter and decorator, because they are at the very heart of your business.

Tip 19: Stay informed on your competition

We live in a competitive business environment. There's always someone out there trying to one-up you, or take your customers away. This isn't out of malice, they are just doing the same thing as you – trying to make the most money possible by providing the best service possible. With this in mind, you need to try and stay ahead of your competition. Check their websites, what are they saying and doing? Could you offer a better service?

Could you be more competitive? When I send a quote, I always add in the email, "I like to stay competitive, so if you receive a more competitive quote please forward it over and I'll see what I can do". If you make a good first impression, then the odds are very high they'll do this for you. I would rather give a discount providing I'm still making a profit than lose a job to another firm. I've seen so many of my competitors' quotes now because this seems to always work for me.

Tip 20: Get your advertising right

Personally, I've found that my website, Checkatrade, MyBuilder and the PDA have been the most successful for advertising my business. This could be different for you, but you won't know till you try. Having a website that stands out from the rest is crucial. I'm lucky, because I was granted permission to use professional images from a £20m house I painted when working for another company, to use on my website. Be sure to spend money on a good website. It doesn't have to be complicated, it can be simple and to the point, but has to look great. Invest in signage for your van or car. Purchase some advertising frames or boards to leave outside the property you're working in or screwed onto the scaffolding. Avoid scams from fake magazines and companies that call asking for payment. Before making any payments, ask them to email more info first. Avoid emails asking you to tap on the link to view work plans, personally I would always delete those emails right away.

Tip 21: Always carry business cards

Carry business cards everywhere, because everyone is a potential customer! I leave a business card with everyone everywhere I go, whether I'm visiting a department store or a restaurant, you never know who might need your services. You could also leave them with other tradesmen you meet at site, or with the many people you meet during your day. You've got nothing to lose by doing this, and trust me when I say that putting yourself out there can reap huge benefits.

Tip 22: Get your recruitment right!

If you are running a business, then it's imperative that you get your recruitment right. Later in this guide, I will provide you with a chapter on how to craft a CV. This chapter will also be useful for the business owners amongst you, as it will show you what makes a good candidate.

When looking for painters and decorators, I look at their personality as much as ability. Personality is obviously important, as these people will be representing me and the business I've worked so hard to build. They will come into contact with my customers, and bad attitudes will harm my business. This is unacceptable and cannot be allowed. So, it's important to make sure you hire the right people.

Tip 23: Get your payments right

Really this is down to personal preference, but it's still important that you get this part right. I like to organise payments from customers in instalments as the job progresses. I normally take a percentage upfront as a deposit, then another halfway through, and the rest on completion. Depending on the scale of the job, this is usually ok. It protects against and prevents too much of a loss, should the worst happen and the customer is not able to pay for whatever reason. Ultimately you should do what you feel most comfortable with, but it's important to have safeguarding measures in place in case things go wrong.

Tip 24: Register with project hubs and contract portals

Project hubs and contract portals are a fantastic way of finding working. By registering, you'll get emails when there are local contracts available. This is normally better if you are a limited company, and represents a great way to stay in the loop and find out what opportunities are available locally and nationally.

Tip 25: Spray!

In my opinion, spraying definitely makes sense. I recently invested in the all new Graco ultra-cordless handheld spray gun. I'm so glad I did, as it looks and feels amazing, it's an easy and economical way to apply paint. Airless spraying is up to 4 times faster than brushing or rolling. I used it on very detailed coving, which would have taken ages dabbing and stabbing the bristles of the brush in every nook and cranny. The sprayer completed the job with absolute ease, just passing over the surface with a couple of swipes. This great machine produces an even coat of paint on all types of surfaces, leaving a high-quality finish. It's also very versatile, using a wide range of paints including interior and exterior jobs. No thinning of the paints is required, paint can be used straight from the tin which is great. At only 2.38kg the Graco handheld Ultra can easily be moved around to complete any small job. I say small job, because the cup attached to the gun only holds 32 0z, so it wouldn't make sense to try spraying a wall or ceiling, because you'll constantly be filling the cup back up.

For larger projects like exterior pebble dash, masonry or interior ceilings and walls there are larger sprayers. There are 2 types of spraying machines – HVLP and Airless. HVLP paint sprayers (High-Volume, Low-Pressure) have an air compressor that atomises the paint. The downside is you'll have to thin the paint to the right consistency, which can be a pain. In the case of airless sprayers, a piston is used to pressurise the paint through a small orifice, and there's no need to thin the paint.

What Is A Painter and Decorator?

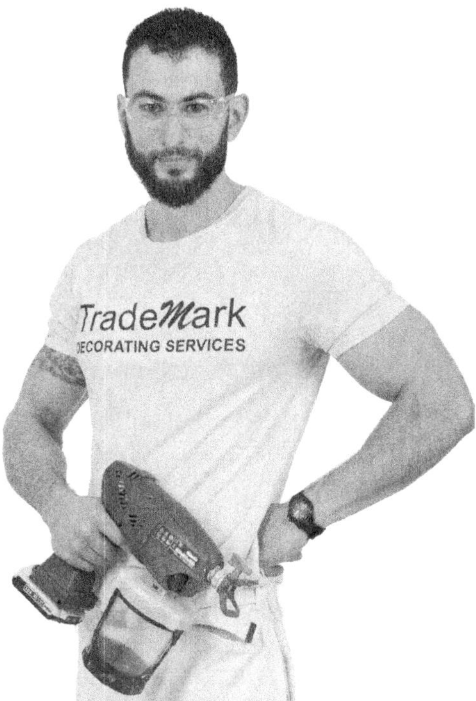

What is a painter and decorator?

In a nutshell, the role of a painter and decorator is to prepare and apply materials such as paint or wallpaper to different surfaces. This is putting it extremely simply, as there is obviously a lot more to the job than just that! Typically, you'll be asked by your employer to visit a site and then begin work based on a set of specifications or instructions. Jobs for painters and decorators can really vary. Whether you are redecorating a home or working outdoors, you can guarantee that every single day will keep you active and on your toes.

Common tasks done by painters and decorators can include:

- Stripping wallpaper, to be replaced with fresh wallpaper or new layers of paint.
- Using primer and undercoat to cover up a surface.
- Mixing paint, sometimes using computer software to establish the right shade.
- Cleaning your equipment after each use.
- Performing key safety and maintenance checks on worksites.

The requirements to become a painter and decorator are not as strict or set as in other careers. There are plenty of ways to get started in the career, whether you start as an apprentice, or take a college course in painting and decorating. When it comes to initial training, you can enrol at a local college and take an NVQ City & Guilds. If you're working for a company, then you can have an assessor visit you on site. This can be paid for by your employer, so it's definitely worth enquiring. Otherwise it'll cost you around £2000 to £3000 depending on what NVQ level you're going for.

If you are intending to work on a construction/building site, then you will usually need a Construction Skills Certification Scheme (CSCS) card. Your qualifications will show on your CSCS card. The colour card you receive will depend on the level NVQ you successfully passed. CSCS cards are mandatory if you wish to work on commercial sites, you'll need to pass the health and safety test in order to receive this card.

Should I fly solo, or work for someone else?

This is a big question for many tradesmen. Do you work for someone else, or become self-employed? The majority of this book is designed around helping you to secure a job with someone else, but if you do decide to go solo then there are lots of advantages to this.

For some people, being self-employed makes perfect sense, as it allows you to be your own boss. You can work flexibly. However, it also comes with enhanced responsibility. If you are your own boss, then you need to deal with issues such as tax and insurance.

With this in mind, I think it's important to really think hard before you decide to become self-employed. There are so many things to take into account, and questions to ask yourself. This includes:

- Do you have the capacity to attract clients on your own?
- Do you have a business plan?
- Once you do start attracting clients, how are you going to expand your client base?
- Do you have enough money to cope during 'dry periods'?

Along with the above, you also need to think about factors such as space, and equipment. Working for an employer comes with many benefits, such as sick pay and paid holiday leave. So, if you are very new to the industry, then it might be worth picking up some more experience before you set out on your own.

What qualities do I need to become a painter and decorator?

While the requirements to become a painter and decorator are not strict, I do strongly believe that you need to be a certain type of person to succeed within the industry. You'll need to be able to demonstrate what is known as the **core competencies**. If you aren't familiar with this term, it basically refers to the core behavioural requirements of a person within the trade. For example, being organised. These competencies are really important, as they serve as a guideline for how you should carry yourself within the industry. Here's the core competencies that you'll need, in order to become a successful painter and decorator:

Customer Service

Customer service is incredibly important for any painter and decorator. Whether you are running your own business, or working for someone else, it's essential that you can treat customers with respect and dignity. Remember that customers are the backbone of any painting and decorating business. Without customers, there wouldn't be any work at all, so it's very important that you can establish a rapport with them. Customer service incorporates qualities such as being polite, respecting the rules of your customer's home, being punctual and respecting customer wishes.

A person with good customer service skills will:

- Communicate politely and effectively with customers, establishing exactly what they require and giving them a reasonable timeframe for the job.
- Respect the rules/expectations of the establishment in which you are working. For example, offering to take your shoes off when entering a customer's home.
- Ensure the customer understands exactly what work is being done. If there are any issues, makes sure that these are raised immediately.
- Following completion of a job, will ensure that the customer is 100% satisfied with the work that was done.

Organisation

It's incredibly important to stay organised when working as a painter and decorator. This is one of the most difficult things for newcomers to do. The role itself requires you to carry around a great deal of equipment, which means that you'll need all of this equipment when you are on a job. Therefore, it's important to stay organised. It's no good getting to a job, only to realise that you don't have half the materials or equipment that you need, because you are disorganised. This will annoy the customer and delay the work.

A person with good organisation skills will:

- Ensure that they stay on top of what equipment is needed for what job.
- Complete jobs on time, and within the agreed quality requirements.

- Plan ahead of schedule, to ensure that they can arrive for jobs on time.

- Ask the customer key questions, to establish the exact needs and requirements for each job.

Attention to detail

When working as a painter and decorator, it's very important that you can demonstrate good attention to detail. During my time in the industry, I have met hundreds of different painters and decorators. While many of these people were fantastic professionals, and great at their job, some of them were not so good. The most common quality I spotted amongst those who didn't perform so well, was that they had poor attention to detail. As a result, their work was extremely sloppy. They failed to take pride in their work, and it really showed.

A person with good attention to detail will:

- Ensure that every piece of work is done to the utmost perfection and quality.

- Notice when things are not being done correctly, or when there is a potential problem, and respond accordingly.

- Take pride in their work.

- Review the quality of their own work, and make conscious efforts to improve where possible.

Adaptability

Adaptability is a really crucial part of working as a painter and decorator. At the end of the day, no matter how well you plan for a job, there are always unexpected elements that come up. For example, you turn up to the job and the client isn't home that day, meaning you can't enter the premises. Suddenly you and your staff are left without work for the day. Or, you turn up to start a job, only to discover that a leak has totally destroyed the room that you were meant to be decorating. Now, you'll need to do extra prep work beforehand. The challenges of this role are endless, and there's no telling what each day will bring. A good painter and decorator can think on their feet, and adapt to cope with ever-changing conditions. Being adaptable means that you won't let bumps in the road prevent you from completing a job successfully.

An adaptable person will:

- Remain calm and composed in the face of setbacks and adversity.
- Take steps to inform the customer of new solutions and ways to deal with problems.
- React flexibly to problems, taking into account that new solutions will need to be found.
- Encourage their co-workers to think flexibly and reactively about new or unexpected issues.

Communication

This ties in with customer service, and it's a major competency to have. Your communication skills need to be top notch. Unfortunately, you would be surprised to hear that this isn't as common a quality as you would think within the trade. I've met many fantastic painters and decorators. These people had a great grasp on their craft, and they were flexible, innovative and dedicated...with one just caveat – their communication skills were terrible. The problem is that even if you are fantastic at the job, you need to be able to communicate with customers. Whether you are self-employed or working for someone else, you are representing the company. It's all too easy for customers to look at a worker who doesn't speak much or just grunts at them, and think 'that person is rude', before jumping to negative conclusions about the company. You don't have to be a people-person to work as a painter or decorator, but you do need to try and make an effort to interact with the client. Be polite, considerate and friendly to them. This is so important to me, that I try and make a real effort to train every single one of my staff in communication skills. I want them to be a friendly face, when representing my business.

A person with good communication skills will:

- Keep the customer informed about work progress, and take an honest approach to any setbacks that arise.
- Try to build a friendly rapport with the customer, helping them to feel comfortable about allowing workers into their home or building.
- Maintain good relationships with co-workers, to ensure maximum efficiency.
- Clearly communicate with team members, ensuring everyone is on board and understands the task at hand.

Teamwork

Teamwork is a vital competency to have. This isn't just the case for the painting and decorating trade, but for many others too. If you are working for a painting and decorating company, then it's very likely that you'll be paired up with at least one other person for jobs, and depending on the scale of the project you may also be working with an entire team. A team can only run efficiently if all of the members of the team are working in sync with one another. Disharmony and disagreements within a team can quickly derail things, and will ultimately harm the customer, because the work will suffer. With this in mind, it's vital that you are a team player. You must be someone who can get along with others, take into account the views and opinions of different people, and value the needs of the group over the needs of yourself.

A person with good teamwork will:

- Make an effort to build rapport with the other members of the workforce.
- Listen to, and take into account, the views and opinions of other members of the team.
- Put the needs of the team over the needs of themselves.
- Support and encourage the other members of the team in completing work as efficiently as possible.

Taking pride in your work

The final competency on this list is having the ability to take pride in your work. There are lots of different titles for this competency, but it all boils down to one thing – doing the best possible job! Nobody can do a great job if they don't care or take pride in the work. You need to be enthusiastic and dedicated to the task. This means actually caring about the work you are doing. It means putting in the effort to ensure that the work is as good as it can possibly be.

A person who takes pride in their work will:

- Make sure that no job is complete until the customer is 100% satisfied with the work that has been done.
- Take a positive and enthusiastic approach to the work they have been set.

- Ask for tips on improvement, to better their work for the future.
- Always be looking for ways to enhance their quality of service.

Core competencies are not just important for when you get the job, but they are also a crucial part of most job application processes. When you interview for a job, many of the questions will be 'competency-based questions'. What this means is that you'll be asked questions such as 'Give me an example of a time when you've demonstrated great communication skills'. You'll then need to answer, showing the interviewer that you have used communication in the past to resolve an issue, and that you could do it again in the future. The competencies will also be important when constructing a cover letter and CV. Now, let's get into that.

Applying For Jobs

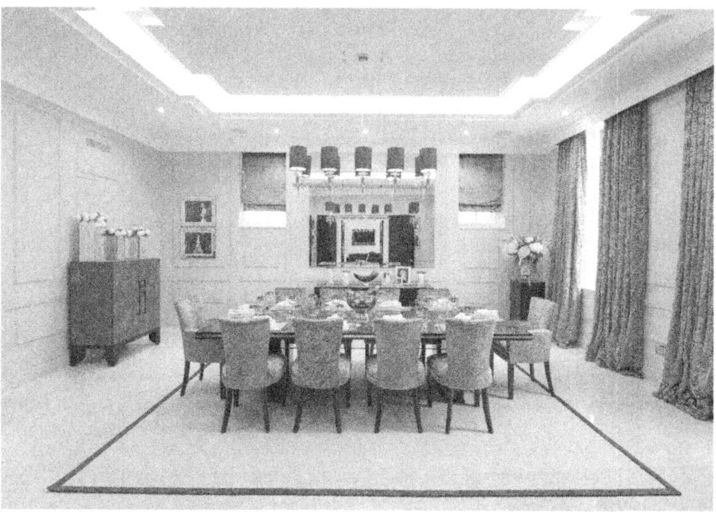

We all have to start from somewhere. If you are a beginner to the trade then naturally you won't be thinking of starting your own business right from the get-go. Instead, you'll be looking to secure a job with an already existing-employer. In this chapter, I'm going to give you some advice on applying for jobs as a painter and decorator. The advice contained in this chapter will also be really useful if you are an employer, or thinking of starting your own painting and decorating business.

Selling Yourself To Employers

So, you've finished your training, and you're now ready to start looking for jobs. Where do you start? Well, naturally the first place to look is the internet. A quick google search should provide you with information on jobs in your local area. There are always companies looking for skilled painters and decorators, so have a good look around to see whether there are any job descriptions which really suit you. Once you've found a job, it's important to read through the entire description thoroughly.

Below I've included a sample job description. This is typical of the type of thing that you can expect to see when applying for jobs online:

Painter and Decorator Needed

Location: Ficshire

Salary: £16,000 pa

Working Hours: Wednesday – Saturday, 7am-4pm

We are an established brand, working in the town of Ficshire. We are looking for an experienced painter and decorator to join our renovation team, on a full-time basis.

During your role, you will be responsible for supporting the renovation team in ensuring that their clients' needs are met to the utmost satisfaction, and ensuring that all work is done to the maximum quality.

Your duties will include:

- Assisting the management team with daily maintenance tasks. You will be working under the guidance of our painting and decorating specialist.
- Ensuring that the workplace environment is safe and clean at all times.
- Using the correct tools and equipment to ensure that all work is done to the maximum quality.

Candidates for this role must have the following qualities:

- Fantastic attention to detail.
- Great customer service and communication skills.
- An affable personality, easy to get along with and enthusiastic for the tasks at hand.
- The ability to take pride in your work.

While previous relevant experience in painting and decorating is preferable, we are happy to take on candidates who can show training and knowledge of the role.

If you feel you meet the criteria for this position, then please send your application to the following email address: Paintinganddecorating@ficshire.com

How To Break Down This Application

When you read a job application, you need to be able to break it down – filtering out the essential details. The reason this is important, is that it will allow you to tailor both your cover letter and your CV to the job description. So, looking at the above job application, we can see the following core requirements:

'Supporting the renovation team in ensuring that their clients' needs are met to the utmost satisfaction.'

Here you can see the core competencies of **customer service** and **taking pride in your work.**

'Assisting the management team with daily maintenance tasks. You will be working under the guidance of our painting and decorating specialist.'

Here you can see the core competency of **teamwork**.

'Ensuring that the workplace environment is safe and clean at all times.'

Here you can see the core competencies of **organisation** and **attention to detail.**

Using the above approach, go through the rest of the application. What other competencies did you find? You should have spotted that in essence, this application asks for every single competency mentioned earlier. Basically, the company is looking for a dedicated and professional painter and decorator, who can work with the team, and shows the utmost care and enthusiasm for the task. Make sure you pay close attention to the responsibilities listed, because this should give you a very good idea of what the company is looking for. Think about the tasks they've listed, and what type of qualities you would need to complete them. For example, 'Assisting the management team' would require someone who is affable, professional and has good communication skills – as you'll need to listen to your senior managers and take on board their advice.

Now that we've established the key points of the application form, let's look at how to create a cover letter for this job.

Writing A Cover Letter

Cover letters are a really important part of any job application process. A cover letter is a short letter, that you attach to your CV, when sending it off to companies. Your cover letter should be 3 or 4 paragraphs in length, and it should basically introduce you and who you are to the organisation. In your cover letter you should talk about topics such as:

- Your background.
- Your key strengths.
- Your interest in the organisation.

When constructing a cover letter, it's incredibly important that you pay close attention to grammar, spelling and punctuation. As someone who reads cover letters on a regular basis, from applicants who want to join my company, I can tell you that if I receive a cover letter that is riddled with errors – I'll just chuck it in the bin, and I won't even bother to read the CV either. There's just no point, because what does that say about the person? Submitting a cover letter that hasn't been checked and proofread tells me that the person applying a) doesn't care enough about the job to do this, and b) has poor attention to detail. These are not qualities that I would want from any of my employees.

Below I've provided you with two sample cover letters, both written in response to the job above. See if you can spot which one is most likely to get the job.

Cover Letter 1

Alright mate,

I saw your application on internet and wondered if you would give an interview? I've got loads of training, been working for painting and decorating companys for a while now and I think I'm the right person for the job because I've got loads of skills that would be great for your company. I applied for job because the pay is really great and I think that would be really beneficial for me. Your company could definitely use someone like me because I looked on internet and saw some propa terrible reviews so I think I could help you out. I got lots of skills, really useful.

Cheers,

Chris.

Cover Letter 2

Dear Sir/Madam,

I am writing to apply for the role of painter and decorator. I came across your application on the internet, and I believe that this role would be the perfect position for me.

In terms of my skillset, I am an organised, creative and hardworking individual, who has recently completed a level 3 NVQ City & Guilds. I'm looking for a role where I can refine my skills, and become a truly great painter and decorator.

Upon researching your company, I was highly impressed by what I found. I discovered that you have a wealth of positive reviews online, some of which showcased your work. I know that you have around 20 or so experienced employees, and I would really welcome the chance to learn from these individuals and hone my craft. I am someone who finds it extremely easy to get along with everyone I meet, so I have no doubt that I would fit right into your team.

I really hope that you will consider my application. Thank you for taking the time to read this.

Yours sincerely,

Chris.

Put yourself in the position of an employer. Which of the above cover letters is most appealing to you? Obviously, the answer is the second one. Not only does the first cover letter contain lots of mistakes, but it's also poorly written, doesn't take a formal tone, and comes across as quite self-indulgent. In contrast, the second cover letter is grammatically correct, and well-written. It politely highlights the individual's skillset to the employer, as well as showing a great level of respect towards the organisation. You should always start a cover letter with 'Dear Sir/Madam' and finish with 'Yours sincerely'. This is the formal and correct way to address someone in a position of authority, who you have not met. Likewise, the second cover letter shows that the individual has researched the organisation and highlights qualities that he likes. This shows enthusiasm and dedication, and as a result this person is much more likely to receive an interview, or at the very least for the employer to move on and read his CV.

Now that you've seen how to go about constructing a cover letter, let's move onto your CV.

What is a CV?

CV stands for curriculum vitae. A CV is basically an organised collection of all your skills, educational and work experience, and your key strengths, all collected in one very neat form. The way you lay out your CV is really important. This is cliché, but it's estimated that most employers will look at a CV for around 20 seconds in total, and if they can't find the information that they are looking for in that timeframe, then they'll simply discard of it altogether.

When it comes to analysing CVs, I'm a little bit more lenient than I am with cover letters. In my opinion, there is no excuse not to get a cover letter perfect. You have just 3 or 4 paragraphs, so there aren't any layout issues to take care of. All you need to do is focus on the basics. CVs are a bit trickier, because putting all of the information into an organised format can be difficult. I don't think that there are too many people who actually have a good idea of what should and shouldn't be in a CV. Yes, you can find numerous examples of how to layout your CV on the internet, but often these will provide conflicting advice. That's why, in this section, I want to give you a really clear idea of how to go about presenting your CV. Remember that not every employer will be as lenient as me, and many employers will expect nailed on perfection. So, it's important to get this right!

Laying out your CV

There are many different sections to a CV, but there is one rule that I think should be followed almost religiously – keep it 2 pages in length. Anymore than 2 pages in length and you are going to struggle to keep the attention of the employer. Remember, employers don't have time to read through every single CV that they receive in complete detail. They need to be able to glean the information they need in a very short space of time. With this in mind, here are the different sections that I recommend you divide your CV into:

- At the top of the page, include your name, home address, telephone number and email address. **TOP TIP**: Your email address matters! You need to use a sensible sounding email address. So, that old Hotmail address that you used when you were 14 is not going to cut it. Stick to something sensible such as JohnSmith1982@gmail.com, and avoid email addresses such as SexyJohnny1982@hotmail.com, because these will make you sound extremely immature and childish.

- Next, you need to write a personal profile. This should be a very short and succinct summary of who you are and what you can offer.
- The third section should be a 'skills and qualities' section, essentially explaining your strengths and what you could bring to the company
- Following this you should include a section on 'educating and training', where you list your school grades and any training you have completed.
- After this, you should include a 'work history' section, where you list your different roles and what your job was at that company. **TOP TIP**: Keep this section relevant. You don't need to list every single role you've ever had, just the ones which utilise the skills needed for this job.
- Finally, you should complete the form by giving a short paragraph on your hobbies and interests, and finally include some reference details. **TOP TIP**: Play it safe with your hobbies and interests. If you tell the employer that your favourite hobby is to visit the casino and gamble your earnings away, then they are unlikely to be impressed.

On the next two pages, we've provided you with a sample CV, for a painter and decorator. Take a look at this and see how it compares to your own.

Sample CV

104 Ficshire Road

Ficville, Ficshire

105 3AD

09909990999

JohnSmith1982@gmail.com

John Smith

PERSONAL PROFILE

I am an extremely ambitious, hard-working and motivated painter and decorator. As someone who has a real enthusiasm and interest for the painting and decorating industry, I see myself as the perfect fit for this position. I know from reading the job description, and researching your company, that this is a role which requires a great team worker, attention to detail and dedication to the task.

I believe that I could bring all of these qualities, and much more, to your organisation. Therefore, I would be very grateful if you would consider my application.

SKILLS, QUALITIES & ACHIEVEMENTS

I believe that my skillset is perfectly attuned for this role. Having studied the art of painting and decorating from a very young age, through my father, I feel that I can combine the tips and experience I have picked up here, with the lessons learned from my NVQ City & Guilds, and my apprentice with Workwood UK.

In the past three years, I have worked for an established local painting and decorating company. I started out as a junior in this company, and have swiftly risen up through the ranks, until I became a supervisor within the organisation. This role required me to take leadership of large scale projects, and manage the work of other painters and decorators. I was highly successful in this role, and I put that down to my hard work ethic, and my knowledge of the trade.

My fantastic communicational skills allow me to deliver a fantastic service to all customers, and in turn this allows me to act as a fantastic representative of any company that I am working for.

EDUCATION AND TRAINING

Ficshire College

- 2005-2008
- NVQ Level 3 City & Guilds

Ficshire High School

- 2000-2008
- A-Level Design and Technology, A grade. A-level Mathematics, C Grade. A-Level English, C grade. A-Level French, C grade.

- GCSE Design and Technology, A Grade. GCSE Mathematics, C grade. GCSE English, C grade. GCSE French, B grade.

EMPLOYMENT

2014 onwards

Supervising Painter and Decorator for *HomeCare Solutions*

Responsibilities: Managing and overseeing work on various local projects, working with apprentice decorators to improve their skills, enhancing the reputation of the business by building connections and rapport with customers and potential clients.

2012-2014

Painter and Decorator for *HomeCare Solutions*

Responsibilites: Working with an established team of painters and decorators, on various local projects. Was required to maintain an organised approach to work, dealing directly with customers and with senior members of staff.

2008-2012

Apprentice Painter and Decorator for *Workwood UK*

Responsibilities: During this time I worked for an established UK company, earning my apprenticeship and learning tricks of the trade. I assisted experienced painters and decorators in their daily work, and was eventually trusted to take on projects of my own, representing the company.

INTERESTS AND HOBBIES

I am a very active person. In my time away from work, I participate in running events, and have previously taken part in marathons. I keep to a regular training schedule, and also enjoy swimming. I am part of a swimming club, which trains at weekends.

REFERENCES

Available upon request.

Hopefully the above CV should give you some idea of how to lay out your own. You should be able to see how I've kept everything in the CV relevant and on point. Almost every single line has some relation to the job that we'd be applying for, and there's absolutely no unnecessary information. If you looked at my CV and wanted to know my key skills, there they are, and the same for any other element. Now that we've covered how to apply, let's look at some top tips for painting and decorating.

Painting

Top Tips

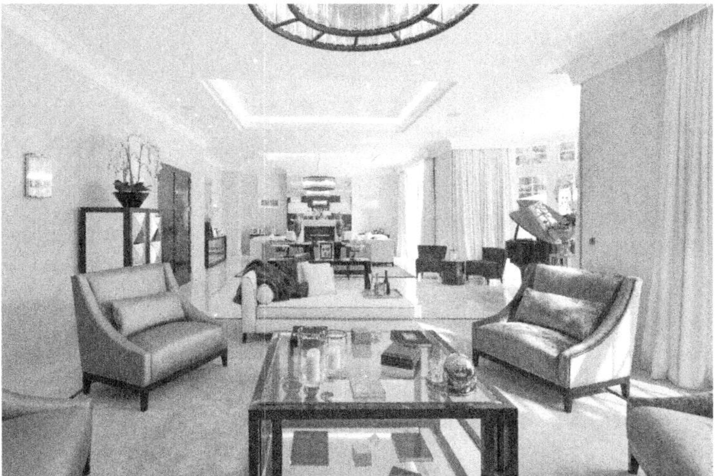

Although this book is largely designed to help you apply for, and successfully get, painting and decorating jobs, I also want to share with you my wisdom about actually working within the trade. As someone who is highly experienced, I believe that the tips and advice I can give you – on a wide variety of topics, could prove very useful. So, in this chapter we'll cover some crucial information on painting.

Your Equipment

Before you start any job, it's vital that you can make sure you've got the right equipment! You don't want to be left high and dry, panicking, because you failed to bring the correct tools to a job. This will cost you time and money. So, with that being said, here's a quick guide to the tools that you should always have to hand when starting a job:

Prepping

Sand paper	**Roll on floor protection**	**Masking tape**	**Plastic sheets**
Sand paper	**Filling knives**	**Scraping knives**	**Wallpaper stripper**
Stanley blade	**Wallpaper steamer**	**Hammer**	**Screwdriver**
Tape	**Wire brush**	**Caulk gun**	**Power drill**

Painting and Decorating Tools

Brushes: mixed sizes	Handheld paint spray gun	Paint sprayer	9-12-18inch rollers
Mini rollers	Tape	Sash brushes	Kettles
Scuttles	Angle brush	Artist brushes	Extension Poles

Getting The Right Paint Finish

One of the most important areas to get right as a painter and decorator, is getting the right paint finish. If you get this wrong, then you'll end up wasting substantial amounts of money, whether that's your employer's money or your own money. As a general rule, if you are painting kitchens, bathrooms, hospitals or nurseries, then you could aim for a higher sheen. The reason for this is that sheen is directly related to shine. The higher the sheen, the higher the shine. Higher shine is more durable, and therefore provides better quality. On the other hand, if you don't want a really shiny effect, then you can simply choose a lower sheen level. There are durable matt paints that can be used instead. There are downsides to using a higher sheen too, such as the fact that a higher sheen will also bring out imperfections in the wallpaper or wall structure. Along with this, you also need to consider the cost, because higher sheen can also equal more expense.

You'll hear terms such as 'sheen' bandied about a lot in the trade, along with terms such as flat-matt (which has no shine at all), and silk – which is 100% shine. There's also gloss and satin, both of which are useful in their own way. Confused yet? Don't worry. Here's a handy overview of how I allocate different paints to different buildings or rooms.

Orhan's Pro Painting Guide!

In this section I'm going to tell you about the different types of paint that I commonly use and where you can use them.

I use the following paint finishes on wood and metal, which also come in exterior versions.

Gloss is a high-sheen finish and reflects lots of light, giving a lovely contrast to walls painted in matt. The surface will need to be well prepped to make it look its best. When applied over a couple coats of undercoat it's a tough old finish, and can take a serious beating, so you are better off using gloss on areas made of wood and metal that are likely to come into physical contact with people – such as windows, doors and handrails. Generally, you should avoid using gloss on walls, because it will literally show up every single inconsistency or roll. Gloss comes in oil or water-based versions.

Satinwood comes in oil-based and water-based versions. It's for wood and metal and is super durable too, it's a low-sheen finish. Although it doesn't match up to the same high level of sheen as gloss, it is now the most popular finish for woodwork as I use this on virtually every job.

Eggshell

Eggshell gives a beautiful classic look to woodwork and can also be used on walls when you want a heritage style look with a tough finish. It's a subtle-shine finish, which doesn't stand out too much. The biggest advantage of using eggshell is that it does a fantastic job of covering up the inconsistencies that finishes like silk can't. Generally, you would use eggshell in an area such a dining room.

I use the following paints on ceilings and walls.

Flat Matt is for walls and ceilings, it gives a beautiful velvety rich, flat finish with excellent opacity. This is the best paint to use if you're looking for that contemporary or period feel. The reason for this is that matt soaks up light rather than reflects it, meaning people's eyes won't be drawn to any inconsistencies there may be on the wall! The disadvantage of matt is that it's not particularly durable, and this means that it's hard to clean. You are best to use matt in rooms which won't be impacted by rough contact with people. So, while adult bedrooms are a good choice for matt, children's bedrooms are a definite no-no.

Matt Emulsion is a high opacity velvety water-based paint for painting walls and ceilings. Matt emulsion dries to a flat matt finish and doesn't reflect light, so any small imperfections won't show. This paint can be applied with a brush, roller and spray.

Vinyl Matt is a finishing top coat. It is like matt emulsion, but has vinyl added to make it tougher. As a result it has a very slight sheen, so imperfections may be seen.

Diamond Matt is the Dulux Trade version of a washable paint, not the cheapest out there but probably the best.

Silk usually has less opacity, in which case it's better to apply a base coat of matt emulsion in the same colour beforehand. Silk dries to the highest-sheen finish which can be scrubbed down, so it is very popular in hospitals, schools, kitchens and bathrooms. I often also use the matt finish kitchen and bathroom paint from Homebase or B&Q. It's cheap and good quality. This is useful, as not everyone likes the sheeny finish produced by silk.

Masonry Paint is for exterior use. It creates a tough, flexible, and very durable finish. It's high opacity and will protect against weather. Used for pebbledash, brickwork, rendering and concrete, bare surfaces will need stabilising solution before any painting to seal and protect the substrate.

Painting Techniques

Before applying any paint to surfaces, you should take into consideration the sequence of the task at hand. Make sure that a wet paint edge is kept at all times, and your work doesn't get damaged in any way. If you are working in someone's home then you may need to work around them.

Normally you should begin by painting ceilings, working from one end of the room to the other. When cutting in the ceiling, it's good to come down the wall a little, so that you have a nice clean line to cut into. Once dried, apply the next coat. The walls should be next. You can cut in the entire room, then roll the walls after for the first coat, and then go wall by wall for the final coat. For the last coat, you should aim for the paint to dry together at the same time, to avoid patches. Next is the woodwork: doors, frames, skirting boards, windows, dado rails and picture rails. This would usually be the correct sequence, however with experience and taking into account different circumstances on different jobs, you may change the order to what suits you best.

How to hold a brush

Generally, the closer you hold the brush to the bristles, the greater control you'll ultimately have. So, the further away from the bristles, the less control you'll have. You should hold the brush around the ferrule/stock. This is the metal band that connects the handle to the bristles, with 3 fingers on one side and a thumb on the other, with your little finger on the back edge.

Hold your finger close to bristles for 2/3 inch brushes, similar to how you'd hold a pen. It would be a massive advantage on difficult to reach areas if you could use both hands.

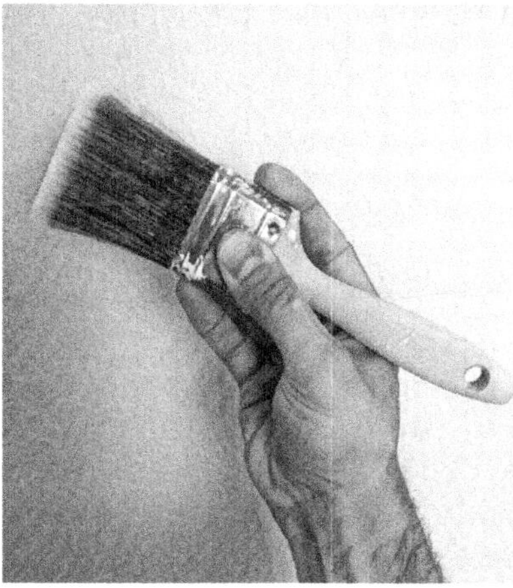

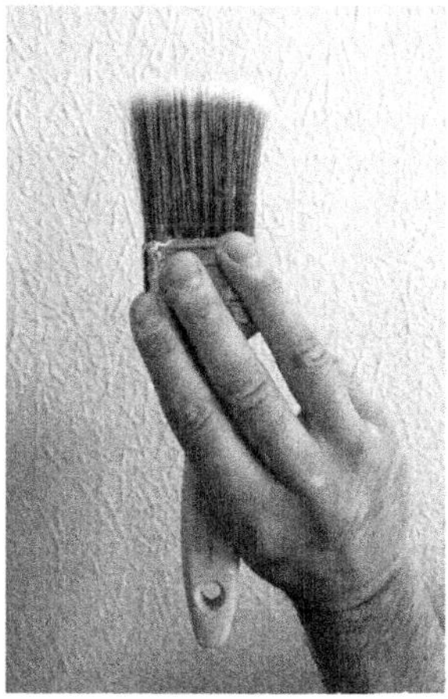

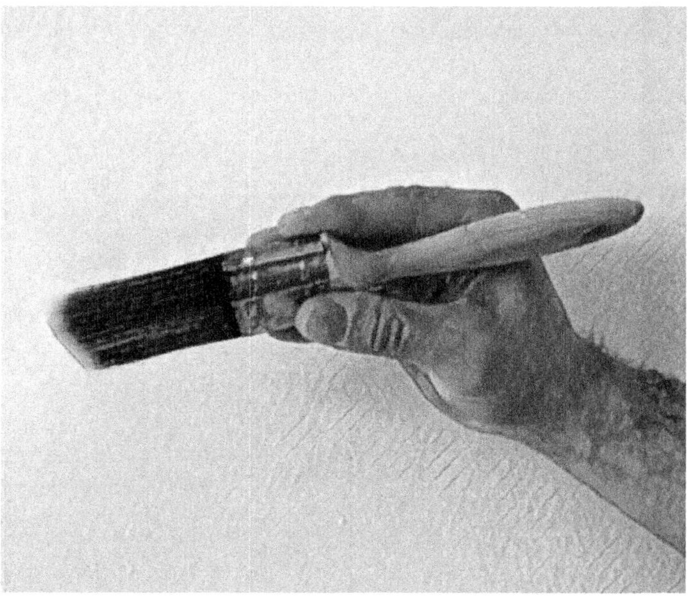

How to cut in

Cutting in means that you use a paint brush to paint areas that are too tight for rollers. This helps to produce a sharp neat line between two structural components like a wall/ceiling, architrave/wall or wall/skirting board etc. When I cut in either on a ladder or on the ground, I get myself comfortable, stable and supported first. I normally keep my breathing very controlled, holding it in at times. If you can keep yourself still whilst cutting in, and a steady hand helps too, then you'll find it a lot easier. Wearing a headlight will really help you to see the line clearly if visibility is poor.

I normally commence with the top left-hand corner of a wall/ceiling by wiggling the brush into the corner very gently. A little vibration is all that's needed to release the paint into tight corners. I then work to the right-hand corner, applying pressure to fan the bristles slightly, so as to use the tip and spread the paint in a straight line. Don't worry about getting a perfect line on your first pass, as you can get it on the second or third, practice will make you better. Using a mini roller to go over the paint area will eliminate any brush marks, and also feather the edge.

Be sure to use a paint kettle and liner too. Using a kettle limits contamination to the paint tin, and liners will save you time washing/wiping the kettle out.

Dip the bristles about halfway, then pat (don't wipe) both sides of the brush on one side of the kettle, leaving the other clean to lean your brush on when taking a break.

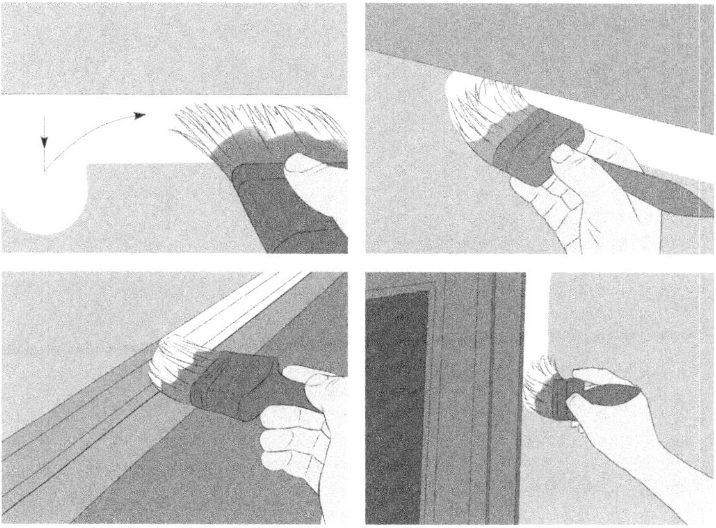

Using a mini roller

I use a mini roller to go over the line I've just cut in, because it will eliminate brush marks. It will also eliminate the halo effect that different textures could have after rolling the entire surface with a big roller. Mini rollers come in short (used to apply oil or water based paint to smooth surfaces), medium and long (used to apply water based paint like masonry to rough areas) pile versions and are also used to apply paint to small areas – such as flush doors, door panels, behind and around radiators, window reveals and other smaller areas that the big roller won't fit in. Once you've rolled the head of the roller in the paint, taking care not to get any on the frame, apply it to the surface without lifting the roller away until it's evenly spread.

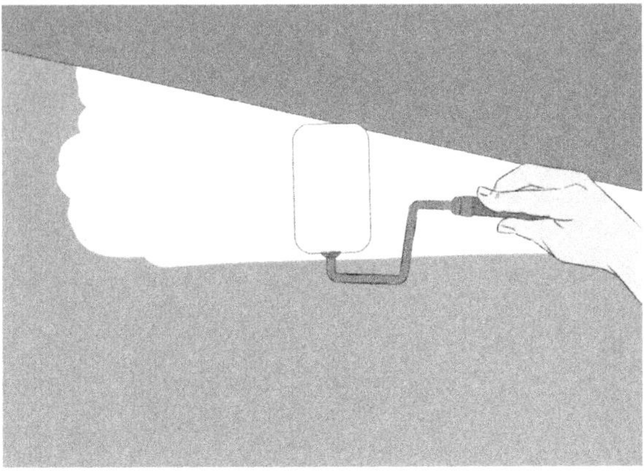

Using a roller

Rollers come in a variety of sizes, but the most common are 9,15 inches, depending on how large the surface is that you need to paint. Using an extension pole will help a great deal to comfortably and safely reach all areas.

When you are rolling ceilings, always take care to apply the finish coat in one direction. This will help you to avoid different looking textures that could result in creating different shadows, which will look messy.

I normally work rolling in squares about 4 feet by 4 feet, keeping a wet edge at all times. Always think about where natural light is coming from, where the windows are, and roll towards the wall of the light source. You are more likely to see lap marks if they go across a light source than towards it. If there is no light source, then you can pretty much roll in any direction, as long as it's the same direction.

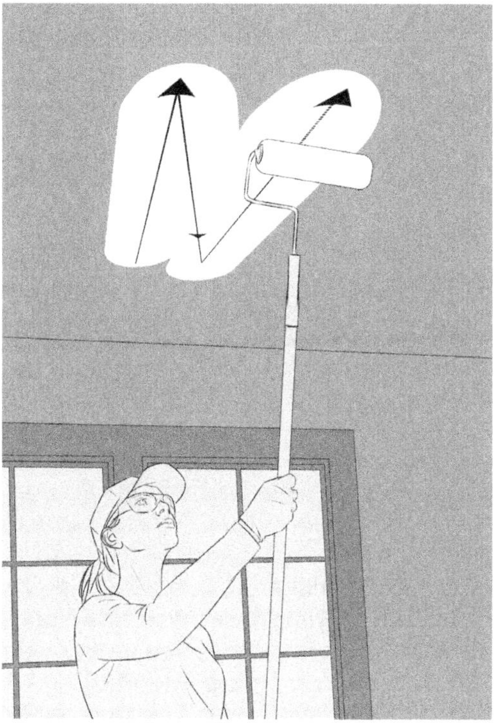

When rolling walls, begin at either the right or left side. I use an extension pole and roll from left to right. Once the roller is fully loaded with paint, twist the roller around as you lift it to prevent drips, then make contact with the wall in the middle and about a foot or so from the edge. Roll up and down, spreading the paint evenly to the lines that you should have already cut in around the edges. You can apply some pressure to begin with, but once the paint is even, roll back lightly to leave a smooth finish. Repeat the process until the wall is fully coated. Once you commence rolling, always finish the wall and square off, because otherwise you will end up with lap marks.

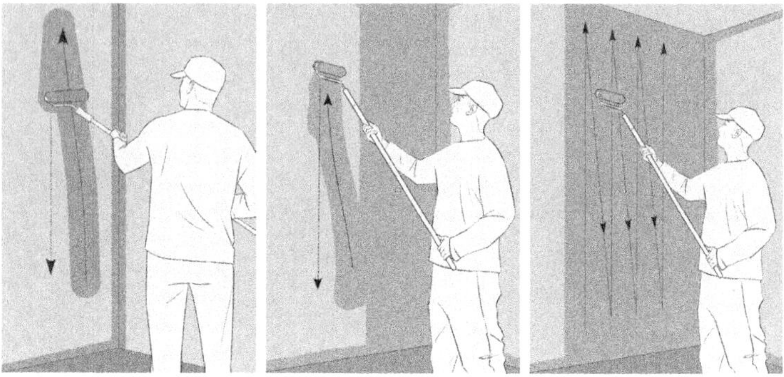

Caulking and filling

You will use caulk and filler as much as you will paint. Caulk is used for areas prone to shrinkage and movement, so cracks and holes filled with powder filler or plaster surfaces may split open. Caulk is waterproof and a sealant. It is used to fill cracks, gaps, joints and voids that are around 3/8 of an inch wide or less. The surfaces should be clean, dust free and painted. Cut the tip of the caulking tube to the size and angle depending on the width of the crack or gap you're trying to fill. When the caulk tube is in the skeleton or caulking gun, hold it at a 45-degree angle to the crack being filled. It's better to pull the caulk along, rather than pushing when filling, as pushing results in an uneven and messy bead. Apply steady pressure on the trigger, to stop the flow release and pull back the rod behind the cartridge if it has one. With a clean, lightly wet cloth, small sponge or finger, pass over the entire applied bead of caulk to smooth, finish off and push into the gap between substrates. Leave to dry completely before painting over with water-based paint, otherwise cracks will appear all over the caulk beads. This is because the water-based paint dries much quicker than caulk, and by the time the caulk dries out it cracks the already dry paint. This normally doesn't happen when applying oil-based paint onto wet caulk though.

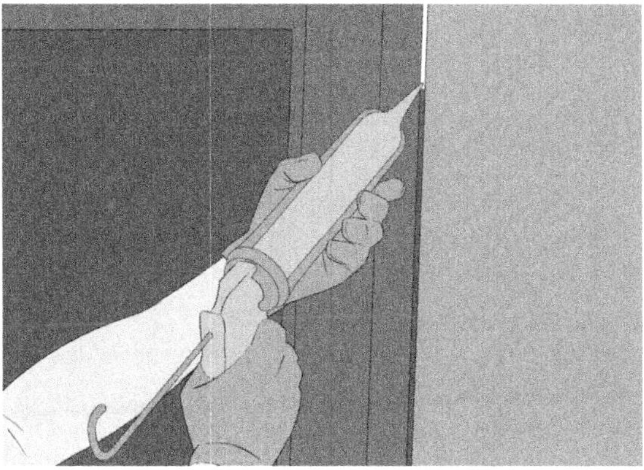

When filling with powder interior/exterior filler for walls and ceilings, the surfaces should be clean and free from any flakes of paint, grease or dust. Once you've followed the instructions on how to mix the product with water, or maybe you opted for the ready mixed type, you'll want to end up with a smooth whipped-cream like consistency. This isn't too runny, yet it's not too thick either, so it should stick to the filling knife if you turned it upside down. When you're filling, always leave a tidy flush finish, because when it dries you'll have to sand it down. Wood filler comes in two parts. To find the correct mix, I use the comparison of a golf ball size of filler, to a pea size of hardener. This stuff reacts, and goes hard quick, so you need to work quickly. If you haven't used this filler before then make sure you wear gloves.

Brush or Spray?

Whether you use a paint brush, a roller or a spray, there are plenty of options available. However, part of being a great painter and decorator is in knowing which tools to use in which situations. It's important to get this right early, because when you are planning for the job, you'll need to take into account the exact equipment that's needed.

Below I've given you a run through of the advantages and disadvantages of painting and spraying.

Paint Spraying

There are a multitude of advantages to paint spraying. It covers a wider area in a short range of time, and could only require one coat. Along with this, it also leaves a really smooth finish. Finally, if you are brushing it can be really hard to reach certain spots, like tight ceiling corners. Spraying solves this issue.

Despite this, there are also some downsides to spraying. While paint spraying is a pretty fast way of working, the actual planning and prep work can take a long time. You'll need to take care to put down layers of masking tape, and cover up areas that you don't want sprayed, because naturally the spray will leave marks on the entire surrounding area. In line with this, it's fair to say that spraying doesn't quite have the consistency of brushing. It's really easy to leave lighter and darker patterns on the surface, just because the consistency of the spraying is difficult to get right. Finally, there's the fact that spraying uses up more paint – which is more expensive in the long run.

Brush Painting

There are lots of reasons for why brush painting is great. Primarily, brush painting gives you more control. Ultimately it's your skill with the brush that will determine how well the job is done, because you control where the paint goes. This means that you can apply the paint more evenly, to give a more consistent finish. Likewise, if you do the job properly then brush painting is less expensive than spraying.

Despite this, there are some downsides, namely that brush painting is slower. It requires less prep-work then spraying, but at the same time is subject to factors such as human fatigue and error. It's a much more meticulous process than spraying, and can often require two coats of paint, but ultimately it will save you paint in the long term.

How about both?

Before we finish this section, just a little note on a technique I'm particularly fond of – back brushing. This is essentially a mixture of both painting and spraying. First you spray the area, then you brush over the wet paint. This creates a consistent layer of paint, and allows you to do the best possible job on areas that are super hard to reach. Usually the technique is as follows: spray, then back brush, then spray once more.

While back brushing is great, you should really only do this when the job really requires it. The best example of where to use back brushing, is if you are painting somewhere that's been weather-beaten, such as an outside wall.

Wallpaper

Top Tips

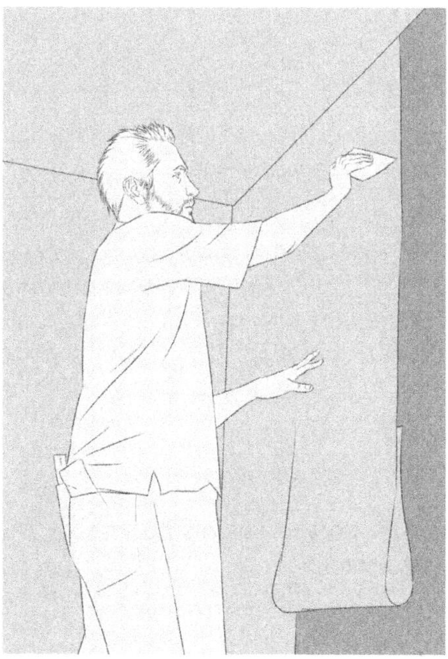

As a painter and decorator, wallpaper is an essential part of your trade. The right wallpaper, when done well, can add a stunning finish to the walls of any room. Whether it's a bold, colourful patterned wallpaper, or a subtle, neutral wallpaper, it's important to get this part right!

In order to do a great job, you'll need to consider elements such as:

- Measuring and cutting wallpaper to the correct length.
- Hanging the lengths, to achieve a straight and smooth finish, on walls, corners and stairwells.
- Applying adhesive to wallpaper.

In this chapter I'll provide you with some top tips on how to make sure your wallpaper is first class!

Your Materials

To begin, let's have a look at the materials that you'll need when you're given a wallpaper job.

- Wallpaper (naturally).
- Wallpaper adhesive. This is also known as wallpaper paste. Before using a wallpaper paste, it's extremely important that you ensure you've got the correct adhesive. If the wallpaper is high-grade, then you'll need heavy-duty adhesive.
- Overlap and border adhesive.
- Small nail. This holds the plumb line in place. Usually I would use a wire nail.

- Wooden batten. A batten is a thin piece of wood. The function of this is to stop the paper rolling up whilst the adhesive is applied.
- Scaffold board. This is used when you are wallpapering a hallway with a high ceiling, or a stairwell.
- Rope. This is a safety measure. It secures the platform that you are standing on to the ladder.
- Large cloth. Using a cloth is important, as it protects the wall from ladder related damage. Just wrap it around the ladder.
- Duster. You'll need to dust before wallpapering, especially behind areas such as radiators.

Now that we've looked at your materials, let's look at the tools you'll need:

Wallpapering Tools

Dust sheets	**Step ladder**	**Combination ladder with stair function**	**Plumb line**
Claw hammer and screwdriver	**Long spirit level**	**Wallpaper cutting guide**	**Ruler**
Paper hanging brush	**Wallpaper smoother**	**Pasting brush**	**Pasting table**

Tape measure	Pencil	Wallpaper scissors	Utility knife
Seam roller	Bucket	Large sponge	Radiator paint roller

Before you begin, make sure you remove any existing wallpaper from the room, and clean the walls too. This will give you a smooth finish. It's also essential for helping you to avoid air bubbles – which can cause creases when hanging new wallpaper.

Measuring and Cutting Wallpaper

Measuring your wallpaper correctly is essential, as it helps you to avoid wasting paper. Measure the wall at your starting point, from the ceiling to the top of the skirting board.

Step 1

First of all, measure the height of the wall, using a tape measure. You'll need to take as many measurements of the wall as possible, especially if it's a larger area, since not all walls are completely straight. I recommend adding 100mm to the measurement. This means that you have an 'allowance' for any unforeseen variations in the height of the area, and it can easily be chopped off later on.

Step 2

Next, unroll the paper on the pasting table. Make sure you do this pattern-side down. Following this, draw a line (using a ruler) with a pencil across the entire width at the measured point.

Step 3

Cut the first length. You should use wallpaper scissors for this.

Step 4

Turn the cut length over, and then unroll the next length. Place this edge-to-edge with the first length. Now match the pattern. Use the first cut length to cut the second length. Continue cutting several lengths following this.

How to apply adhesive to the wallpaper

Step 1

Mix the wallpaper adhesive. Read the instructions on the packaging carefully, as this will tell you how to go about doing so.

Step 2

Next, lay the cut length down on the pasting table, with the paper hanging over the edge of the table. Place it pattern-side down. If it keeps rolling up, then use a batten to stop this from happening. Keep the long edge against the edge of the table.

Step 3

Now, apply the adhesive. You should place this in the centre of the sheet, then brush it towards the edge that's lined-up with the end of the table.

Step 4

Work the adhesive on the edges of the paper. Between lengths, wipe any adhesive spills off the table with a wet sponge.

Once the first half is completed, line up the opposite edge of the paper with the other side of the paste table. Paste outwards from the centre again.

Step 5

When the paper has been pasted, fold it over. When doing this, do your best not to crease it. Following this, start a concertina. Move the concertina to the end of the table, using the batten to stop the unpasted end from rolling.

Step 6

Apply adhesive to the entire length, folding the paper as you go. Set the concertina aside, to allow the adhesive to soak into the paper. The paper needs time to expand before it is hung. This process is known as soaking. It prevents bubbles appearing as the paper continues to expand.

Step 7

Apply adhesive to a few cut lengths, for one wall.

How to hang the first length of wallpaper

When hanging the first length, it's best to start at a corner. Hang the first length of wallpaper on a wall that has no doors or windows. This will allow you to hang a full length, from the ceiling all the way to the top of the skirting board. Work away from windows, so that the paper edges will not cast a shadow when overlapping.

It's really important to get the first length of wallpaper right. If it's not straight, then the next lengths of wallpaper won't be straight either, and it will snowball into an almighty mess.

Remember too that walls and corners are rarely straight, so don't rely on them as a guide when hanging paper.

How to hang the first length of wallpaper

Step 1

First of all, check the width of your lining paper. Note this figure down, and then subtract 50mm. This will allow for an overlap. Measure the remaining width (from the edge of the wall) and mark it with a pencil.

Step 2

Next, hammer a nail into the wall near the ceiling. Put the nail in line with the first mark, and then hang the plumb line from this.

Step 3

Mark the wall down the length of the line, then join the marks up, using a ruler.

Step 4

Position the first length at the top of the wall. Keep the right-hand edge running down the vertical line. Don't forget about the overlap. Hold the paper at both sides. Be careful not to let it tear or stretch.

Step 5

Use a paper hanging brush to smooth down the wallpaper. This should help to remove any air bubbles. Whilst doing this, make sure the right-hand edge stays on the pencil mark.

Step 6

Use the back of a pair of wallpaper scissors to crease the top of the paper against the ceiling junction. Pull the paper away from the wall, and then snip along the creases with the scissors. Brush the edges back into place. TOP TIP: Occasionally dip your scissors into a bucket of warm water. This stops them getting clogged with wallpaper adhesive.

Step 7

Finally, finish with the skirting boards. You should use a wallpaper cutting guide for this. Hold the guide against the skirting board and then tuck the paper into the crease. Finish by trimming the paper, which can be done with a utility knife.

Sockets and Switches

Top Tip: Dealing with sockets and light switches is a tricky subject, and something that I always get asked about. Luckily, I have some great tips on how to get around problems here. For a start, make sure all the power is turned off before you start working around these – because otherwise you'll be in for a nasty shock (no pun intended!)

When wallpapering around sockets and light switches, hang the paper as normal, and go straight over the switch/socket. Be gentle when you're going over the fitting, as you don't want to tear it. Hole the paper, and then mark each corner using a pencil. Then, draw lines going into the centre, from each corner.

Make a hole in the middle, cut along the lines you've drawn, and then pull back the flaps. Once you've done that, unscrew the faceplate (but only partially so) and then pull slightly away from the wall. Now, you can put the faceplate gently through the hole in the paper, before brushing the edges, and screwing the plate back into place.

Once that's done, let the paste dry, and turn on the power again. Simple!

External Corners

When wallpapering corners, I recommend taking the following approach:

First of all, be sure to paste carefully along the top of the wall and skirting. Once you've done that, you can line up the length, so that it goes around the corner with the previous length. Make sure you don't stop at the corner though, and follow all the way round, using an overlap of 3 inches – this makes pasting the next strip easier. Take the wallpaper brush and smooth the seam down, before securing the corner strip. Once you arrive at the corner, make a relief cut – height-wise, down the top of the corner of the wall, and fold the paper over. Wrap around the corner, smooth the paper, and then trim the overlap along the ceiling. Do the same process with the bottom of the corner that meets the skirting board, maintaining the process of smoothing the wallpaper out with a brush, and then follow round to where the overlap ends. The same goes for internal corners, but be sure to push the wallpaper into the corners properly.

Doorways

Wallpapering doorways is similar to windows. When wallpapering doorways, you should start by hanging the wallpaper from the top, and then smoothing it down – all the way to the top of the architrave. Using scissors, cut the wallpaper from the top of the architrave into the corner-edge of the architrave. Once you've done that, push the paper into the angle and down the vertical edge. Finally, use a smoother against the crease, and trim the overlap.

Windows

This is very similar to doorways. First, hang the pasted wallpaper as normal so that it overlaps the actual window and sill by a few inches. Then you can start by cutting the wallpaper around the sill, by feeling where the edge of it is, and then cutting into towards the edge width-wise from the top corner, then the bottom corner. Once that's done, use a smoother to push the paper into the angles of the wall, architrave and window sill.

Reveals

When it comes to the reveals of doors and windows, there's a very specific procedure. For either side of reveals, drop a length of wallpaper over the reveal, leaving 3 inches or so over the wall itself. Then, cut width-wise from the top of the reveal until you reach the edge of the reveal, and follow this up by implementing the same procedure at sill level. Fold the paper around into the reveal, and trim to the edge of the window frame. You can finish by hanging the drop to the wall above and below the reveal, trimming at the ceiling and skirting as usual.

For the middle of reveals, continue papering along, being sure that patterns match up. The central drops will fold round the wall into the underside of the reveal – just make sure you shape the edge with a smoother into the reveal. My advice, when doing this, is to use roll ends or off-cuts. These will help with smaller areas.

Once that's all done, your next task is to paper the corners – specifically the ones which haven't been covered previously. To do this, measure out the area which needs to be covered. When measuring, add on 3cm to the top and bottom, and the side which folds against the corner. After measuring, you can start pasting. If you are using a pattern, then at this point you need to make sure that this matches up with the reveal – otherwise you'll get an ugly or disjointed effect.

After pasting, take a wallpaper brush and use this to shape the corners, making sure that you are pushing into the grooves of the reveal.

If you've done the above right, you should end up with creases along the overlaps. You can then trim these, smooth over, and apply the exact same technique to every single corner. Rinse and repeat until the entire reveal has been done – job complete!

How To Ace Your Interview

This is a really important element to master if you want to gain a position as a painter and decorator, so pay close attention.

If you've never attended an interview before, then here's the basic process:

- Usually you'll send the interviewer your cover letter and CV.
- Following this, they'll make contact with you via telephone or email, arranging for you to meet with them to interview.
- Finally, you'll attend the interview.

Initial Contact

Different employers do things in different ways, but the general rule is that you need to make a great impression right from the off. Some employers might ask you to participate in a telephone interview first, prior to attending the face to face process. When the employer makes contact with you, it's really important that you show enthusiasm, commitment and good manners. Let's take a look at an example.

The below letter is from an employer, inviting a candidate to attend an interview with them.

Dear John,

Thank you for your application to HomePaintingUK. We were impressed with your CV, and would like to invite you to attend an interview at our HQ – 31 Ficshire Street, Ficshire, on 6th March at 14:30pm.

Please respond to this email ASAP, to let us know whether you can attend.

Sincerely,

Martha Higgins.

Now, have a look at the two responses below. Which one do you think is better?

1. Dear Martha,

Thanks for your email. I'll be happy to attend. See you at 14:30 on 6th March.

Cheers,

John

2. Dear Martha,

Thank you for your email. I would be delighted to attend, and I really look forward to meeting with you all. Thank you for the opportunity.

Yours Sincerely,

John.

In this case, the obvious answer is that option 2 is better. There isn't anything significantly wrong with option 1 (apart from signing off with 'cheers') but at the same time it doesn't show much enthusiasm for the cause. You might think that small details like this won't matter, but they really do. You need to demonstrate your interest and enthusiasm as early as possible.

Attending Your Interview

So, you've got your date, time and location for the interview. What now? Well, the first thing you need to do is to start researching. One of the most common areas that people fall down in an interview, is that they fail to look into the company to whom they are applying. These days, more and more companies expect their interviewees to have done research, and quite rightly so. Using the internet, you can find out a wealth of information on just about any company, so brush up! Look into the type of work they've done and in which areas. Find out lots of positive things to say, and keep them in mind for the interview.

Next, it's time to suit up. You absolutely need to dress smart for your interview. Regardless of what profession you are working in, interviewers will expect you to turn up looking smart and presentable. You don't need to splash huge money on a suit for an interview, but at the very least you need to make sure that you are wearing a shirt, jacket and tie, with some smart shoes.

Finally, research the route to your location. The worst thing you can do is to arrive late for an interview. Whether it's down to poor planning or bad luck, it will create an absolutely terrible impression of you for the interview. So, research the route beforehand, and if necessary you could even do a test-run before you attend, just to see how long it takes. Try to arrive at least 10 minutes early for your interview, if you can.

Interview Questions

As mentioned, different employers will tackle the interview process in different ways. Some employers will ask you competency-based questions, whereas others will take a more laid-back, generic approach. Some may even ask you a mix. Whatever the question type, it's best to be prepared for every single possible outcome. So, with this in mind, below I've drawn up a list of interview questions, and I've also provided you with a breakdown on how to go about answering these questions, along with a space for you to write down your own answers. The questions below are questions that I would typically ask in an interview, as a business owner and experienced painter and decorator.

Question 1: Tell me a bit more about yourself.

This is the most common starting question for any interview. It seems easy enough, but you still need to be careful when answering it. When they hear this question, many people go off on a big ramble, which doesn't really tell the interviewer what they want to know: who you are and why you'd be a good fit for the company. The interviewer doesn't want to know that when you were 14 you played for your local football team, or that you once broke your leg climbing a tree. They want to know what type of person you are – hardworking, professional, dedicated, and what experience you have in the industry, why you are interested in painting and decorating, etc. You should try to structure your response into three stages: what type of person you are, a short section on your background, and finally link your background to the role that you are applying for.

Write your own response to this question in the textbox below.

Question 2: Why have you applied for this role in particular?

This is a question which ties together your research with your reasons for applying to the position. Here, you need to tell the interviewer about what you've discovered when researching their company, and give some positive feedback on this. For example, 'I know that your company is highly prestigious, and was awarded a certificate on excellence at last year's National Renovation Awards. I would be honoured to work for a company as esteemed as this.' Obviously, try to keep it realistic. A company will know if you are just flat out exaggerating to try and flatter their ego. For example, telling a local painting and decorating firm that it's been your dream to work for them ever since you were a child, is going to raise a few eyebrows. Keep it relevant, but still complimentary.

Write your own response to this question in the textbox below

Question 3: What is your biggest strength?

You can usually expect to hear this or 'what is your biggest weakness?' during an interview. It's a classic question, as it puts the interviewee in a tough spot, and reveals a lot about their character. For this question, you just need to pick one quality, and then expand on it. Don't go off on a big tangent about all your strengths, because that will just make you sound arrogant. Focus your answer, picking a strength which is relevant to the job you are applying for. For example, you could tell the interviewer that your biggest strength is in your attention to detail, and that you know this would prove useful to their company, because it would allow you to produce fantastic quality in your work.

Write your own response to this question in the textbox below

Question 4: Give me an example of a time when you have demonstrated great customer service.

Here we have a competency-based question. This question is asking you to describe an occasion when you have used the core competency of customer service. When answering a question like this, it's important that you structure your response. You will need to go into detail, and this means that your response will be pretty lengthy. The more structure, the better, because otherwise it could just come across as a bit of a rambling mess! Start by telling the interviewer what the situation was, and then move into what you did to resolve it. Finish up by telling the interviewer about how your behaviour resolved the problem, and what you learned from this experience. Remember to show the qualities that go into good customer service – such as communication and decision making, in your response.

Write your own response to this question in the textbox below

Question 5: What do you think is the most important quality for a painter and decorator to have?

This is an interesting question, which indirectly tests you on the core competencies, and how well you've studied the job description. You could use any of the competencies that we mentioned earlier in this book, but what's important is that you can expand on this and show why they are imperative to the role. You also need to demonstrate that you have this competency! So, don't just say, 'Teamwork is the most important quality'. Tell the interviewer that you believe teamwork is the most important quality, and that you are a fantastic team player, with a high level of experience in working with teams and other individuals.

Write your own response to this question in the textbox below

Question 6: Do you have any questions for me?

You've done it! You've finally reached the end of the interview. That fantastic new job is within touching distance, you can almost reach out and grab the contract...but there's one final hurdle to overcome, and it's this question. Many people completely underestimate the value of this, and your answer can tell the interviewers a lot about you. Don't answer with 'no'! Asking questions at the end of an interview shows a high level of enthusiasm and interest in the role. It shows that you are interested to know more about the company and the position, and that you actually want the job. It shows that you are thinking long term, and not short term.

Here's some questions that you might consider asking:

- What type of training will I receive?
- What would you say are the biggest challenges of this position?
- What is a typical day like working for this company?
- What type of people will I be working with?

There's also some questions that you should definitely avoid asking. These include:

- What's the pay for this role?
- How much holiday do I get per year?
- How long do we get for lunch every day?
- How long until I can get promoted?

Overall, as long you prepare thoroughly, you should be in an ideal position to secure your job with a painting and decorating firm!

Setting Up On Your Own

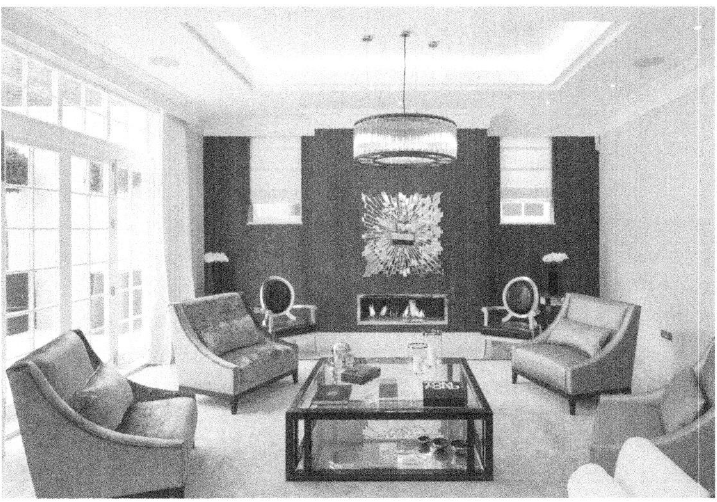

Starting out on your own can be a scary and tricky prospect. Many people ask the question, how exactly do I get started? Where do I even begin? In this chapter, I'll hopefully answer all of your questions.

The Different Types Of Company And How To Register

Sole Trader:

The simplest way to start up a business is to register as a sole trader. What this means is that you individually are the business, and will operate on your own. One of the biggest benefits to this approach is that you will take home all of the profits, and will be free from any registration fees. Of course, the downside of this is that you will need to be extremely responsible, and must maintain a healthy record of all your own accounts. The best way to do this is normally to employ a bookkeeper, or an accountant, who specialises in your area of business. You are also responsible for any debts that the business incurs. This makes sole trading fairly risky, but extremely lucrative if you get it right.

Registering as a sole trader could not be easier. Simply go online, download and fill in a CWF1 form from the HMRC website. Once that's done, and sent off, you will be officially registered as a trading business.

Partnerships:

Running a business as a partnership means that 2 or more individuals will share the responsibility. Together, they will be responsible for all of the costs, risks and decisions made by the company. The biggest benefit of this approach is that it allows 2 or more people to have a say in how the business is managed. Anyone who is listed as a partner with the business will be held responsible for debts incurred by the company, and will be listed as self-employed.

When working as a partnership, the partnership itself has no legal value outside of the individuals in it. If one of them should leave, go bankrupt or even die, the partnership will be immediately dissolved. However, this does not necessarily mean that the business itself will collapse, as the other partner(s) can continue to trade using the company.

Setting up and registering a partnership

There are 3 different types of partnership:

General partnership:

A general partner is normally someone who has invested in the business, and from that point onwards is heavily involved in the day-to-day operations of the company. This person will take a share of the profits, whilst agreeing to be liable for any debts incurred by the company or partnership. This means that each partner could stand to lose even more than they have originally invested, should the partnership run into difficulty. It is a legal requirement for every single partnership to have at least one general partner.

Sleeping or dormant partners:

This is the name for a partner who invests money in the business, but does not then take an active role in the day-to-day management of the business. Similarly to general partners, sleeping partners are still responsible for any debts incurred by the partnership.

Companies:

Companies can also be registered as members of a partnership. If this happens, then the company in question will have all of the same rights and responsibilities as the other partners in the business. If a partnership consists only of companies, then the partnership will be required to create 'partnership accounts', and send their details to Companies House every year. The individuals who are responsible for representing the companies in the partnership will need to include this, when they send their own company account details to Companies House.

Limited Liability Partnership (LLP):

An LLP consists of a number of individual entities or companies, taking shared responsibility for the business, similarly to any ordinary partnership. However, the difference is that the liability of the partnership is only limited to the total amount that has been invested by the LLP into the business, including any financial guarantees that have been offered. If the business runs into financial difficulty, the members of the partnership have limited protection.

Setting up a Limited Liability Partnership (LLP)

Limited liability partnerships will need to meet the same requirements as limited companies, and this can sometimes be very difficult. I'd strongly advise that if you are a non-profit making business, you do not use this structure. In order to register an LLP, you should visit the Companies House website, at www.companieshouse.gov.uk

Limited Company

Limited companies exist as individual companies, and can registered through Companies House. The finances of a limited company are therefore separate from the personal finances of the owners. Shareholders are not responsible for any debts incurred by the company, but could stand to lose out on their original investment if the business runs into trouble.

Setting up and registering a limited company

There are two different types of limited company, Private Limited and Public Limited.

There are a few differences between these two types of company. Mainly, public limited companies are legally entitled to raise funds by selling shares of their company on the stock market. Private limited companies are unable to do this. Public limited companies must also have a share capital of £50,000 or more, with 2 shareholders, 2 directors and a trained/qualified secretary.

At any point a private limited company that is limited by shares can convert into a public limited company, but it must re-register with Companies House in order to do so.

Limited by shares or by guarantee?

Private limited companies are limited by shares, which are owned by shareholders. By doing this, shareholders who have paid the full amount for their share of the company cannot be held responsible for any debts incurred by the business. However, if a shareholder has only partly paid for their share of the business, they will still be held accountable for the amount that they owe for the shares. Private limited companies can also be limited by guarantee. When this occurs, the individuals in the partnership agree on a set liability limit.

In order to register a private or public limited company, you should visit the Companies House website at: www.companieshouse.gov.uk

In addition to registering your private business as a company, you will also need to:

- Clearly display the company name, on the outside of all offices or other places of business;
- Display the company name clearly on all letters, invoices, receipts and cheques;
- Detail your company's registered office address on all business letters and order forms;
- Send all of the necessary registration forms, fully completed, to the Registrar of Companies.

Setting up a Limited company: Registration documents and forms

To register a limited company within the UK, you must send a number of completed forms to Companies House. If you are setting up in Northern Ireland, then you will need to register with the Northern Irish Companies Registry. Here is a list of the documentation you will have to complete and register:

- A Memorandum of Association, providing details of the company's name, location and what it will do;
- Articles of Association. These describe how the company will be run and the powers of the company's directors;
- Form 10 (Statement of the First Directors, Secretary and Registered Office), giving details of the company's registered office and the addresses of its directors;
- Form 12 (Declaration of Compliance with the Requirements of the Companies Act), stating that the company meets all the legal requirements of incorporation.

Financial Management and Organisation

When you start up your new business, time will need to be spent on financial organisation. Having the drive to succeed is paramount to your success. However, poor or no financial management from the onset will adversely affect your business.

The way in which you handle your finances will be critical to the success of your business. If you fail to keep on top of your bookkeeping, then the success of your business venture will be compromised. Conversely, keeping bookwork up-to-date will help you through the lean times and allow your business to grow. One of the most daunting things about starting your own business and giving up full-time work is the prospect of looking after the company accounts.

What to do first

I recommend that before you start trading, you get in contact with the local offices of the Inland Revenue and HM Revenue and Customs. Either call them or make an appointment to see them. You can find a number of useful helplines on the Government's advisory website, using the following contact numbers:

Business Link Helpline

0300 456 3565

Monday to Friday, 9am to 6pm

Business Wales Helpline

0300 060 3000

Monday to Friday, 8am to 6pm

Business Gateway (Scotland)

0845 609 6611

Monday to Friday, 8am to 6pm

Invest Northern Ireland

0800 181 4422

Monday to Friday, 8am to 5pm

When you make contact with the relevant section, explain the details of your business plan and ask them what you need to do. They'll provide you with advice, leaflets and a selection of forms, such as VAT registration that you may need to complete before you begin trading. This is important! If you start off with all the necessary information, it will make the bookkeeping process much easier. It also helps to have a contact within the local offices that you can call whenever you run into any difficulties.

Business Bank Account

In business, it is impossible to survive without a business banking account. Your business banking account will be the nucleus of your finances, and will record every single business transaction. You'll use this account to make payments to suppliers and staff, make withdrawals and other transactions that are integral to running a business. A business bank account will also be extremely useful for working out tax, and can provide you with access to vital support and advice. Before setting up a business bank account, you will need to shop around and take a look at the products and services on offer:

Bank facilities for business owners

- Deposits: Paying in all cash and cheques;
- Withdrawals: Taking out cash through an ATM or a bank branch;
- Payment by cheque: Use of a business chequebook;
- Automatic money transfers: Direct debits and direct credits;
- Night safe: Used for safely depositing money when the bank is shut;
- Balance enquiry and statements: For keeping track of your finances;
- Company debit card: This will debit an amount immediately from your business account, and is free in most cases;
- Company credit card: A payment card that can be issued to important members of staff. There is usually a fee per transaction, an annual fee or both;
- Overdraft and loan facilities: Short-term financing, subject to application procedures;
- Asset finance: Leasing or purchasing facilities to enable you to buy equipment;
- Factoring and invoice discounting: Borrowing (short-term) against the value of unpaid invoices;
- Commercial mortgage: Funding to help you buy a business. Banks will often fund up to 80% of this;
- Deposit accounts: For any reserve funds your business may have;

- Merchant services: This will allow you to accept credit and debit card payments from customers. To get one, you will often need two years' trading history and audited accounts. Upon registration, you will be charged an annual fee, on top of a percentage of every transaction.

An Accountant - Do I need one?

An accountant will be another form of business advisor to you when you first start running your own business. They will be able to give you advice on your business plan and the tax issues of registering a new business. Some accountants offer bookkeeping services, but if they don't, or if you wish to handle this yourself, you can get help with setting up manual or computerised bookkeeping systems. Most importantly, you need an accountant to assist on things such as registering for VAT or PAYE, and the procedures involved.

An accountant will also give you financial advice and help with budgeting, cash flow and credit control, in addition to up-to-date information on any general or legal enquiries.

As your business grows

Whether you are starting up or a growing business, an accountant can advise you on the best way to arrange additional finance without putting your business at risk. Remember, an accountant isn't just there to help you manage your money. Once you have the finance in place, there needs to be some control, in order to ensure that growth of your business is handled in the right way. Many of your concerns will be financial, adequate working capital, good stock control, invoicing and so on – so an experienced accountant's advice will be invaluable in such matters. An accountant will also be on top of all the current taxation issues. Taxation is a large business expense and an accountant can work to effectively minimise these costs.

VALUE ADDED TAX (VAT)

If you're in business, you must register for VAT if your VAT taxable turnover for the previous 12 months is more than £79,000. This figure is known as the VAT registration threshold. The threshold changes – usually once a year – so you should regularly check your turnover against the current threshold.

You must also register for VAT if either of the following applies:

- You think your VAT taxable turnover may go over the threshold in the next 30 days alone;
- You take over a VAT-registered business as a going concern.

VAT quarterly returns must be completed and sent to HM Customs and Excise, along with any overdue payments. Although you must pay VAT on any income generated, you can claim back VAT on some services; such as office supplies, fuel and so on.

Keep yourself up to date with the latest VAT information and rates by listening to the Budget. This will be done by your accountant/bookkeeper, but it is good for you and your business to be aware of this information. Remember that you are expected to account for every business penny spent, and are expected to show each month's profit/loss and income/expenditure in sufficient detail, so that the tax can be clearly calculated.

Accountancy software

Buying an accountancy software package can slash the amount of time and effort spent dealing with your finances. In the early stages, you could use the services of a freelance bookkeeper or your accountant, as mentioned above. This person will already have the software, and will keep your books up-to-date on a monthly basis, for a fee.

Estimates vs Quotes

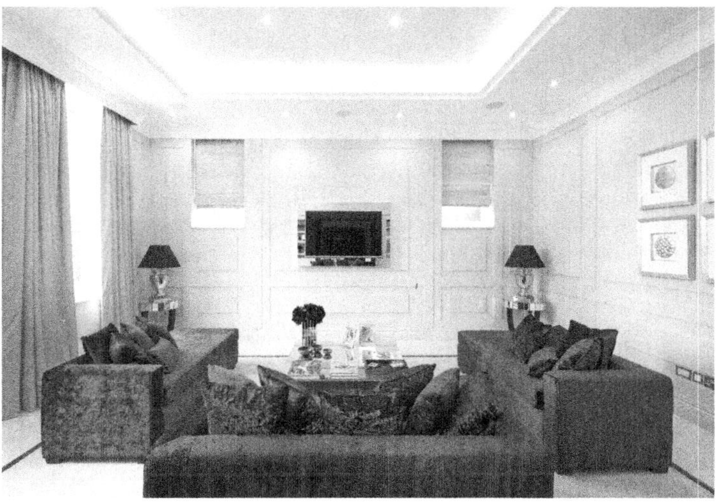

When working as a self-employed tradesman, one of the key things that you need to get right, is the financial element of the business. An important element of this, is quotes and estimates. As you are someone who will be providing each of these in large amounts, you need to understand what these terms mean.

What is a quote?

A quote is an exact price, for a job. A quote is a fixed amount, it cannot be amended or altered once the customer has accepted this – unless the customer changes the initial agreement that the quote was based on. You should only offer a quote to clients when you have attended the site where you'll be working, and established the exact work that needs to be done.

When giving a quote, you should try to think of this as a type of formal contract between yourself and customer. Quotes give the customer confidence, knowing that they won't have to pay out for any extra costs. When quoting, you need to make sure that you pay close attention to detail. Take all of the relevant factors into consideration, before giving the customer a fixed price. Remember that you cannot change a quote, so you need to be absolutely sure of the price before quoting a customer.

What is an estimate?

An estimate is essentially an estimation or guess on how much a job will cost to do. Usually an estimate is given to the customer before you have visited the site, or conducted a thorough inspection of the work that needs doing. Unlike quotes, estimates can change once you have discovered the full scope of the work, or if unexpected occurrences happen whilst you are doing the project. Estimates are more informal than quotes, and aren't to be taken as legally binding.

How do I give my customer the quote or estimate?

Generally, the safest way to give a client a quote or estimate, is in writing. Ideally this should be done using computer software, in a Word document. Save it and send as PDF. This will make your quotes look professional, in comparison to if they were handwritten, which will create a good impression with the customer. It will also make them feel more comfortable about paying you. There is a fantastic website that you can use, called FreshBooks, which will allow you to produce invoices for customers once a quote has been agreed on. You should always keep a copy of your estimates and quotes, as this will be extremely useful to fall back on if something goes wrong or there are disagreements during the process of working. One thing to bear in mind is that you should ALWAYS make sure your customer understands whether you are giving them a quote or an estimate.

What should I include?

So, what should go into your quotes and estimates? Obviously, the first thing should be the cost. If you are giving an estimate, then make sure it's crystal clear on the estimated costs for certain elements of the job, even if these are just approximations. When giving a quote, you need to be really precise and detailed with the exact price of the work and why it costs this amount.

If you are giving an estimate, then I strongly advise that you include a disclaimer at the bottom of the page, noting that the price could change subject to conditions and you fully inspecting the site of work.

Other than the cost, you should also include details such as:

- The date that the quote or estimate is given on.

- The address of the work that will be carried out.
- A short description of what is covered by the quote or estimate, and what is not covered by this.
- The total cost, including VAT.
- Terms and conditions. Terms and conditions are really important, in my opinion. Not only do they cover you in the event of disagreements, but they also make your quotes or estimates look professional. They show that you've carefully thought about your business and the work you are doing, which will reflect better with the customer.

Here is a quote I've used,

TradeMark
DECORATING SERVICES

Quotation #210

Info@trademarkds.co.uk
www.trademarkds.co.uk
07774 604 706
020 34111 106

31/05/2018

Customer details:
Mr ....,
................................,
................................,
....
....

Dear ....,
I have the pleasure in submitting the quote for the following works to be carried out at the property:
Work description:

Internal Painting

Front room

- Tape up door handles, switches, sockets and carpet/skirting board lines.
- Protect floors.
- 2 coats Dulux Trade Vinyl Matt brilliant white to ceiling.
- 2 coats Armstead Trade Durable Matt colour to walls.
- 2 coats Dulux Trade Satin to woodwork.

Downstairs Toilet

- Tape up door handles, switches and sockets.
- Apply stain blocker to area on ceiling.
- 2 coats Dulux Trade brilliant white vinyl matt to ceiling.
- 2 coats Armstead Trade colour to walls.
- 2 coats od Dulux Satin to woodwork.

Kitchen/Diner

- Fill and sand down cracks and holes.
- Tape up door handles, switches, sockets and carpet/skiting lines.
- 2 coats Dulux Trade brilliant white vinyl matt to ceiling.
- 2 coats Armstead Trade to walls.
- 2 coats of Dulux Satin to woodwork.

Hall, stairs and landing

- Protect floors.
- Tape up door handles, switches and sockets.
- 2 coats of Dulux Trade Vinyl Matt Brilliant White to ceiling.
- 2 coats of Armstead Trade Durable Matt brilliant white to walls.
- 2 coats of Dulux Satin to woodwork.

Master Bedroom

- Protect floor.
- Tape up door handles, switches and sockets.
- 2 coats of Dulux Trade Vinyl Matt Brilliant White to ceiling.
- 2 coats of Armstead Trade Durable Matt to walls.
- 2 coats of Satin to woodwork.

Small Bedroom

- Protect floor.
- Tape up door handles, switches and sockets.
- 2 coats of Armstead Trade Durable Matt brilliant white to ceiling.
- 2 coats of Armstead Trade Durable Matt to walls.
- 2 coats of Satin to woodwork.

Labour £2900 Paints/Materials £300

Total £3200

Note: any variations to the work description shown on this quote may result in a variation in the cost.

Yours Sincerely
Mr Orhan Timur Mehmet
Trademark Decorating Services

Conclusion

We have now reached the end of this book. Thank you very much for reading, and I sincerely hope that you have found my tips and advice useful.

I truly believe that painting and decorating can be a lucrative, rewarding and really enjoyable career. Yes, you will need to put in the hard work in order to make the most of it, but if you can do that then you will reap the benefits.

I started from very little, but with experience I have now become a master painter and decorator, with my own highly successful business. Through sheer determination and grit, I have climbed my way up the ladder, and I couldn't be happier with my career choice.

If I had to give you final piece of advice, it would be this: study the core competencies that I have listed in this book. These are the qualities that you will need in order to become successful in this industry. Whether you are starting out on your own or applying for training positions, they will be extremely useful to you. If you are to become successful at anything, then you can't just learn how to do it, but you also need to learn **why** you are doing it. Why does this behaviour impact on the job, and how does it change things? What will this behaviour change, and in what way? Learning the nuanced and subtle details of painting and decorating will separate you from other candidates, and help you become the best painter and decorator that you can be.

Good luck, and I wish you the utmost success in your future career,

Orhan Mehmet.

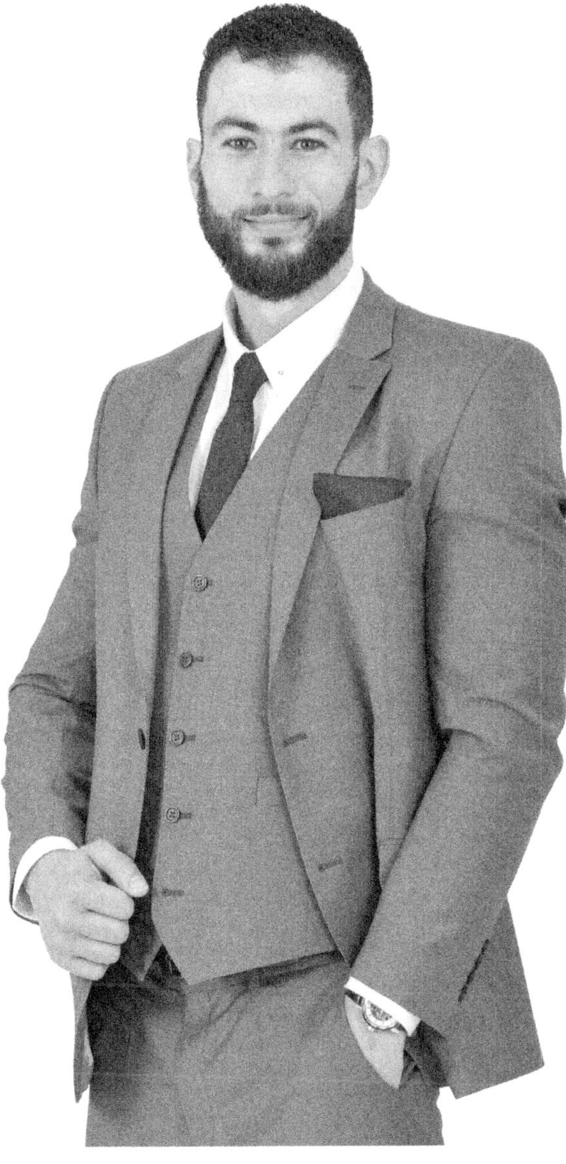

REVIEWS

The following are reviews of my business, from satisfied customers.

"I can thoroughly recommend this company - with full marks for tidiness, reliability, courtesy and, of course, quality of workmanship. The challenge was considerable - not so much a redecoration as a restoration! The end result was remarkable - the house is completely transformed, and the finish was immaculate. I really don't know how Orhan pulled this off, and am genuinely looking forward to working with the company again in the near future."

"Orhan did an excellent job and delivered the end results on-time and to a very high quality. A true professional with competitive prices, Orhan is dependable, trustworthy and delivers as promised. I would have no hesitation in recommending Orhan to all!"

"Very polite, reliable and professional. A very reasonable quote for the work to fully decorate the interior of a 4 bedroom semi. Happily took on additional work requested without any problems. Work was completed to a very high standard and we will be requesting his services again to do the exterior. A pleasure to work with."

"Orhan is a rare professional. His work is perfect: from the assessment of work to be done to completion in high standard, on time and within budget. He carried out painting throughout the flat and the balcony. The colour result was perfect and the flat was left very clean when he finished. I am already looking forward to working again with Orhan."

"I had just bought a flat which had not been decorated for 17 years so there were many holes in the walls, settling cracks, cracks in woodwork, rotten woodwork in shower area etc.

Trademark is very professional, starts early every morning on time every day with minimum of fuss. They gave the flat a complete makeover so now it looks like a new build, smooth walls and wood joints. The paint on walls and woodwork has covered very well and the quality of tiling is very good. I am delighted and would use this company again if I have a new job and would recommend them."

"I have used Orhan's services twice now and would not go to anyone else, I was extremely happy with the work Orhan did and for fitting the job in so last minute for me and being really efficient. He made sure to keep the mess minimal and cleaned away after the work was completed, he was very professional about his work and we are all very happy with the outcome."

"Orhan did a fantastic job with the internal redecoration in the communal areas of my block of flats. The finish is immaculate, he was so neat and tidy in his work and I was so impressed that I've now asked him to redecorate the whole of my flat. First class job, and a very professional service."

"Orhan did a great job. He was totally reliable - starting when he said he would and finishing to schedule. He was willing to be flexible as new tasks emerged during the course of the job. His work was to a very high standard. The house has a lot of wooden beams and Orhan was careful to mask areas to prevent splashes. There were also a number of areas of damaged wall. Orhan did a great job of patching these to get a good finish."

Printed in Great Britain
by Amazon

29643270R00066